Praise for P

"This book is a must read before anyone attempts to preach the pinnacle of wisdom literature called Proverbs. I can scarcely think of a more valuable work to get one started in the right way."

Daniel L. Akin
President
Southeastern Baptist Theological Seminary

"Jon Akin gives a welcome and much-needed corrective to the tendency to preach Proverbs as platitudes, disconnected from the gospel. In this book, Akin teaches how to preach Proverbs and preach Jesus, at the same time."

Russell D. Moore, Ph.D.
President
Ethics & Religious Liberty Commission
Southern Baptist Convention

"If you love the book of Proverbs and desire to expound it faithfully and redemptively, then make this wise choice: read this little book carefully! Jon has served us well by putting countless hours of his study on this particular subject into a very accessible, enlightening, and edifying book. I personally benefited from it greatly in preparing a recent series of sermons through the wonderful book of Proverbs."

Tony Merida
Pastor for Preaching and Vision,
Imago Dei Church, Raleigh, NC
Associate Professor of Preaching,
Southeastern Baptist Theological Seminary,
Wake Forest, NC

"Proverbs is one of the last books of the Bible where one would turn for Christ-centered exposition, and Jonathan Akin has written a thought-provoking and highly readable guide for a Christ-centered understanding of the book of Proverbs."

Matt Carter
Pastor of Preaching and Vision
The Austin Stone Community Church

Preaching Christ
from Proverbs

Jonathan Akin

Preaching Christ from Proverbs

Published by Rainer Publishing
www.rainerpublishing.com

ISBN 978-0692360156

Printed in the United States of America

To Ashley:

"Her children rise up and call her blessed; her husband also, and he praises her: 'Many women have done excellently, but you surpass them all.'"

Proverbs 31:28-29

Contents

Acknowledgements

This book would not be a reality without the help and encouragement of a number of people. Space prohibits me from thanking everyone who has had a part in the production of this work, but I do want to mention a few. I am grateful to the wonderful people of Fairview Church who listened to every sermon I preached on Proverbs with kindness and interest. Their love has been such an encouragement to me. I am grateful to my friend, brother in Christ, and co-laborer Stephen Lorance who took time to edit and proofread this book. His suggestions and insights were very beneficial. I am grateful to my friend Tony Merida who told me I should produce a book on this topic. This book was his idea! It is a joy to teach preaching to pastors in classes alongside Tony. He is a man who models Christ-centered exposition.

I am grateful to my family. My wife Ashley is my best friend. There is no way I would have completed this work without her constant encouragement and prayer. She is a true partner in life who challenges, inspires, and supports me in every facet of my ministry. I also want to thank my young children Maddy, Emma Grace, and Judson. I love them dearly. My hope for them as they grow is that I will teach them the wisdom of Proverbs so that they too can be made wise for salvation through faith in Jesus Christ. I am grateful to my mom and dad – Danny and Charlotte Akin – who imparted this wisdom to me from a young age.

Finally, and most importantly, I am eternally grateful for the Wisdom and Word of God, Jesus of Nazareth. I pray Lord Jesus that you will make me wise, that you will use this book for your glory, and that it might aid pastors in proclaiming you from Proverbs!

Chapter 1

Can Christ Be Preached from Proverbs?

Several years ago, while I was in seminary, some fellow students, a few professors, and I went to dinner with someone considered the Yoda of Christocentric interpretation of the Bible. After dinner we began to ask questions of this renowned scholar. I was in the process of completing my doctoral studies on the Christocentric interpretation of Proverbs, so I was thrilled to get to ask him some questions.

This scholar was not only an expert on Christ-centered interpretation, he had also done extensive work on Proverbs and the Wisdom Literature of the Bible. When it was my turn, I asked, "I get the big picture stuff about how Proverbs points us to Jesus, who is the wisdom of God.

As a Pastor trying to do expository preaching, however, how can someone preach Christ from the details of the text of Proverbs week in and week out in a manner that is both practical and true to the intended meaning of the text?" He sat still for several seconds, and then replied, "Well, it seems to me that in 1 Corinthians Paul calls Jesus 'the Wisdom of God.'" Then, he nodded his head and said, "Next question." I thought to myself, *that's it?* I was discouraged with his response. I walked away from our discussion still confused about how to preach Christ from the Proverbs.

Proverbs is both a fascinating and frustrating book when it comes to preaching. Some expositors shy away from it because it does not lend itself to verse-by-verse preaching. After all, once you get through chapter 9, the remainder of the book appears to be a random collection of truth. Other preachers, however, gravitate to Proverbs because they love the practical, earthy advice and wisdom about daily life. Proverbs seems perfect for the kind of topical preaching that avoids "deep" theology and gives people what they really need—practical tips for daily living in the areas of protecting your marriage, managing your money, and controlling your tongue.

To those who advocate a more gospel-centered approach to preaching, it may seem as if Proverbs is a collection of moral or practical advice that is set apart from Christ and the grace of the gospel. The very reason that drives some preachers to love it – its earthy tone – causes other preachers to avoid it because they do not want to fall unwittingly into the traps of legalism or the prosperity gospel. Are the Proverbs simply the Israelite version of "Dear Abby?" Does Proverbs just give practical advice for us to follow in order to "win at life?" Where is Christ in this book?

These are legitimate concerns for a preacher. Not just because a "Dear Abby" approach to interpretation is often a misinterpretation of the text, which is abstracted from Jesus, but also because such an approach undermines the spiritual health of the church. Preaching the Proverbs as a sort of divinely inspired collection of "Dear Abby" letters will lead to a type of Christ-less moralism that is damning.

For example, consider one of my own sermons from Proverbs. A few years ago I preached a message from Proverbs on the use of the tongue. A man who I knew was lost approached me to tell me how helpful my sermon was. "Your message really hit me between the eyes. I'm going to do a better job with how I talk to my wife." He then turned and walked away. The sermon did not call him to salvation; it only served to make him try harder to be a good husband. This approach to Proverbs is dangerous because it can imply a form of works-based righteousness where people try to earn favor with God by their actions, oblivious to the fact that apart from the gospel they are heading straight to Hell. That is moralism, not gospel-centered preaching.

The other problem with a moralistic approach to Proverbs is that it does not deal with the fundamental issue facing every human being—the cause of our sin. The foundation of our sin problem is not a lack of knowledge; it is the sinful nature we inherit from birth. We are sinful and broken people the moment we enter this world. Even if we learn all the right moves in life because we have mastered the teaching of Proverbs, we still do not possess the wherewithal to obey those principles. This man already knew that he should speak more kindly to his wife, but he fell short when it came to putting that knowledge into practice. All of us do. We are all sinners who have fallen short of God's standard and wrecked our lives in the process. Left to ourselves, we eventually choose the wrong path! We need more than practical tips to change our lives. We need more than moralism to deal with our sin problem. We need *Christ and his gospel*!

Here is where we find good news in Proverbs. The Bible is quite clear that Proverbs is not a collection of divinely inspired platitudes that prepare us to live life in our own strength. The Bible teaches that the point of Proverbs, just like all of the Old Testament Scriptures, is to "make you wise for salvation through faith in Christ Jesus" (2 Tim 3:15).[1] The book of Proverbs ultimately is about the salvation that is available to all in the Messiah, Jesus. The Bible also teaches that Proverbs is a gift to aid us in our sanctification. It is profitable "for teaching, for reproof, for correction, and for training in righteousness, that the man of God may be competent, equipped for every good work" (2 Tim 3:16-17). The *purpose* of Proverbs, just like every other book of the Bible is to save and sanctify those who read it. When we think of preaching through Proverbs, our first goal should be to interpret and apply it the way the Scriptures teach us, in a manner that makes us wise for salvation and molds us into the image of Jesus Christ.

But still, many preachers (and scholars) are skeptical about preaching Christ-centered sermons in Proverbs. Often the opponents of Christocentric preaching use this specific book as evidence that one cannot use all of the Old Testament to preach about Jesus![2] They claim that attempts to preach Christ from Proverbs are contrived and do not deal appropriately with the text. So, the question remains, "Can we preach Christ from the Proverbs?" If so, how? This book will explain how a proper approach to interpretation and sermon development will allow the preacher to proclaim Christ from the Proverbs in a way that unbelievers will know what it means to place their faith in Christ for salvation. This book will also explain to believers how to be further conformed to the image of Christ. Additionally, it includes a summary of the main features of Proverbs, discussion of the main issues related to preaching Proverbs, and Christ-centered sermon notes.

The Structure of Proverbs

Proverbs can be divided into seven major divisions.[3] Grasping the seven divisions and the topics addressed in each will greatly assist preachers as they plan their series through this book.

- Proverbs 1:1-9:18 – The Introduction
- Proverbs 10:1-22:16 – "The Proverbs of Solomon"
- Proverbs 22:17-24:22 – "The Sayings of the Wise"
- Proverbs 24:23-34 – "Further Sayings of the Wise"
- Proverbs 25:1-29:27 – "The Proverbs of Solomon which the men of Hezekiah King of Judah copied"
- Proverbs 30:1-33 – "The Sayings of Agur"
- Proverbs 31:1-31 – "The Sayings of King Lemuel"

An Overview of the Book of Proverbs

The book begins "the Proverbs of Solomon" (1:1). That the book names Solomon as the primary author should come as no surprise. 1 Kings 3 tells the story of how the Lord had given great wisdom to Solomon as a gift. Solomon was the wisest man in Israel's history and in the Ancient Near East (1 Kings 4:30-31). During his life he spoke over 3,000 Proverbs (1 Kings 4:32). While there are other authors mentioned in the book, authors like Agur and King Lemuel, Solomon remains responsible for the majority of Proverbs.

The authors of the book of Proverbs wrote to impart wisdom to "his son," the youth of the nation of Israel. This wisdom is more than a collection of isolated tips on how to make your way through life's difficulties; it is a collection of teachings that instruct us how to restore the harmony among God's people that was lost in Eden. When God created the world, there was peace between God and our first parents, Adam and Eve, peace between Adam and Eve themselves, and peace between our first parents and the created order. The fall of Adam and Eve fractured each of those relationships—with God, each other, and the created order. And the consequences of the fall extend to our lives as well. Proverbs teaches that only when our vertical relationship with God is right—"the fear of the Lord" (Prov 1:7)—can we be in right relationship with others and live in harmony with the created order.

The introduction to Proverbs gives the keys to its interpretation (1:1-9:18). This section has extended instructions from the father (King Solomon) to the son (the crown prince), exhorting his son to commit to the wisdom of the book by having a personal relationship with a person Solomon calls "Wisdom" (1:20-33; 3:13-18; 4:5-9; 8:1-36; 9:1-12). Solomon personified Wisdom as he wrote, implying that Wisdom was one with whom the reader could become intimately acquainted. The father reveals that there are rivals competing for the son's affection like the gang of peers (1:10-19), the adulteress woman (2:16-22; 5:1-23; 6:20-35; 7:1-27), and ultimately Folly herself (9:13-18). Just as Wisdom is personified in Proverbs, so too is Foolishness.

By the end of chapter nine, Solomon has repeatedly admonished his son to marry Wisdom and reject an affair with Folly. It is only possible to walk in the way of the wisdom revealed in Proverbs if one has a personal relationship with Wisdom. The introduction (1:1-9:18) is the key to unlocking the remainder of the book (Prov 10-31). Whether or not you can walk in the way of

Wisdom depends on whether you listen to the voice of Wisdom or the voice of Folly.

The personification of Wisdom pointed to a greater reality than perhaps even Solomon understood, the reality that Wisdom is not a "thing" at all. Wisdom is a person (Prov 1:20-33; 8:1-36; 9:1-6). Wisdom has a name. The Wisdom of God is Jesus of Nazareth (cf. 1 Cor 1:24, 30). Therefore, we may rightly conclude that Proverbs, read through the lens of Jesus himself, is concerned with becoming wise in everyday life through a relationship with the Messiah. If you are not growing in wisdom, it's not because you do not possess the requisite amount of practical tips for life, but because you are not growing in Christ Jesus. Whether you are walking in wisdom or foolishness reveals whose voice you are following. Solomon's point is that the identity of our true master is revealed by the nitty-gritty details of our life. How you use your words, how you work, how you manage your money, and how you treat the poor all reveal whether you are following Jesus in faith or walking away from him in unbelief. If you walk in wisdom, you demonstrate that you are a follower of Jesus; if you walk in foolishness you are acting as an unbelieving idolater.[4]

From Proverbs 10:1 to the end of the book, there are an abundance of proverbs that fit the mold of what someone generally thinks a proverb is—a one or two line pithy saying that gives wisdom for daily life. For example, "Like a dog that returns to his vomit is a fool who repeats his folly" (Prov 26:11). The Proverbs of 10:1-31 should be read in light of the primary emphasis of Proverbs 1-9, walk in the way of Wisdom, not Folly (and the New Testament reveals that personified Wisdom is ultimately King Jesus). These sections contrast the ways of the righteous and wise with the way of the wicked and foolish. How one walks in daily life reveals whether they follow Wisdom (Jesus) or Folly (idols). It is only as you commit yourself to wisdom (chapters 1-9) that you are able to obey the principles of wisdom revealed in chapters ten through thirty-one. This overview of Proverbs gives the preacher a mechanism for understanding how to preach Christ rightly from the book. We will explore the main features of this mechanism in the following chapters.

Chapter 2

Five Christ-Centered
Features in Proverbs

People usually equate wisdom with "street smarts," or intelligence, or having common sense, and Christians often think Proverbs is just the godly version of that kind of common sense. However, wisdom is much more than that in the Bible in general and Proverbs specifically. The next two chapters present ten features to wisdom in Proverbs that must be grasped in order to rightly teach the book to the church. The Bible reveals to us that wisdom is necessary for a king to rule his kingdom, that wisdom is an ability to read people and situations, that wisdom includes ethical discernment of right and wrong, that the only way to be wise in this way is to trust the Lord completely, and that whether one does submit to the Lord and grow in wisdom is a matter of life and death.

The First Feature: Wisdom is Royal and Messianic

The Wisdom revealed in Proverbs has a royal and messianic emphasis. Proverbs teaches that wisdom is the means by which kings rule. Without wisdom, their kingdoms will topple and chaos will arise. Solomon's goal is to train his son in wisdom that their dynasty might endure. Of course Scripture teaches that Solomon's sons falter, paving the way for one greater than Solomon to arise who will establish the Kingdom of God on earth—Jesus of Nazareth.

The Old Testament Background of Royal and Messianic Wisdom

In the beginning, God created humanity to rule creation (Gen 1:26-28), but humanity forfeited their authority by their foolishness. Adam and Eve chose to listen to the voice of the serpent rather than fear the word of the Lord. Proverbs 3:7 teaches that foolishness is being wise in your own eyes. In the Garden, Eve was tempted by what her eyes saw. As a result, she reached for the fruit she thought would give her knowledge of good and evil (Gen 3:1-6). She thought the fruit would make her wise, not the Word of God. Adam's and Eve's foolishness in the Garden (and by extension, all of humanity) made them unfit to rule creation. They abdicated their thrones. Chaos was unleashed upon the world.

Not only is wisdom needed to rule creation, it is also needed to rule a nation well (Isa. 11:1-9; 1 Kings 3:7-9). Deuteronomy equates wisdom with following God's laws (Deut 4:6) and teaches that a king must be a man of the Law in order for his dynasty to endure in the land (Deut 17:14-20). Just as in Eden, successful rule is dependent upon submission to God's Word rather than the pursuit of what our eyes find pleasing. Adam was a king who was not committed to God's Word, the results were disastrous. As the kings and leaders of Israel abandoned God's Law, the results were equally calamitous.

Nowhere is this reality seen more clearly than in Israel's miserable, downward spiral in the book of Judges. Israel literally turned into Sodom and Gomorrah (Gen 19) as a concubine is gang-raped to death, which sets off a civil war (Judges 19-20).[5] Why did this happen? The key refrain at the end of Judges indicates, "There was no king in Israel, and every man did what was right in his own eyes" (Judges 17:6; 18:1; 19:1; 21:25). A refrain repeated in Proverbs to remind us of the importance of wisdom (Prov 12:15; 21:2). Where there is no covenant-keeping, kingly authority over the people, folly and destruction will result. We need someone to save us from and to rule over our appetites and our foolishness lest we destroy ourselves.

God responds to the crisis in Judges by eventually raising up a godly king in David, who is a man after God's own heart (1 Sam 13:14) and keeps the covenant (at least early on). God makes a promise to David that his dynasty will last forever (2 Sam 7). The future of his dynasty is tied in part to the wisdom of keeping the covenant (Psa 89:30-34; Deut 4:6). In spite of the initial descriptions of David, he eventually abandons the way of wisdom and commits adultery with Bathsheba. His son, Solomon, succeeds him and has a promising start to his reign, as well. In a dream, Solomon asks the Lord for a "wise heart" in order to "rule your people, that I may discern between good and evil, for who is able to rule this your great people?" (1 Kings 3:7-9). Just as the book of James teaches that wisdom comes as a gift from God to those who ask for it (James 1:5), God grants Solomon's request.

Solomon recognized that wisdom was essential to rule God's people and to uphold justice by distinguishing between good and evil.[6] The gift of God's wisdom to Solomon's is revealed early in his reign when he adjudicates the issue of the two prostitutes and the baby (1 Kings 3:16-28). God's wisdom enabled Solomon to uphold justice (1 Kings 3:28). The Scriptures teach that the Lord was pleased that Solomon requested wisdom instead of a long life, riches, or victory over his enemies. Because God was pleased with Solomon's request, God gave him long life, riches, and victory in addition to wisdom (1 Kings 3:10-14). Indeed, as Solomon reveals in Proverbs, wisdom is the "pearl of great price" that if sought first will result in long life, riches, and victory. The Lord tells Solomon that if he walks in the Lord's statutes that the days of his life and dynasty will be lengthened (3:14). Again, there is a connection with wisdom, the Law, and ruling authority because the duration of his dynasty is tied to the Law and wisdom.

Wisdom is needed to rule a kingdom well. Solomon's reign is glorious and peaceful because of God's gift of wisdom. His knowledge surpassed that of all the nations around him, so people from all over the world streamed to Jerusalem to hear Solomon's wisdom. As a result, his fame spread (1 Kings 4:34). With this God-given knowledge, Solomon builds the Temple, which is patterned after Eden and the creation.[7] Through the wise reigns of David and Solomon, the Lord was re-establishing human dominion and providing a picture of the coming Messianic Kingdom that will stretch from sea to sea and include all the peoples of the earth (Psalm 72). The reign of Solomon does not last, however, because Solomon loves and marries "foreign" women who turn his heart away from the Lord to idols (1 Kings 11:1ff.).[8] By taking foreign wives, Solomon violated the kingly law of Deuteronomy 17, bringing judgment upon himself and his house. In response to Solomon's sin, the Lord tells Solomon that he will lose his kingdom and that it will be torn apart during the reign of his son. This prophecy is fulfilled when Rehoboam, Solomon's son, foolishly listens to the counsel of his peers instead of the elders of Israel. His foolishness leads to the Kingdom of Israel being divided (1 Kings 12).

Ultimately, Solomon and his sons fail to follow the way of wisdom and break God's covenant. This failure leads to Israel's exile and the toppling of the Davidic dynasty. All hope is not lost, however. The promise of a wise Son of David is given, who by his wisdom will establish an enduring kingdom that lasts forever and set things right in the Creation. The Bible describes this expected king as the embodiment of the wisdom revealed Proverbs. One should note that he is not influenced by what his eyes see:

> There shall come forth a shoot from the stump of Jesse, and a branch from his roots shall bear fruit. And the Spirit of the Lord shall rest upon him, the Spirit of wisdom and understanding, the Spirit of counsel and might, the Spirit of knowledge and the fear of the Lord. And his delight shall be in

the fear of the Lord. *He shall not judge by what his eyes see*, or decide disputes by what his ears hear, but with righteousness he shall judge the poor, and decide with equity for the meek of the earth; and he shall strike the earth with the rod of his mouth, and with the breath of his lips he shall kill the wicked. (Isa 11:1-4 emphasis added; see also Prov 1:1-7).

Ruling Authority in Proverbs

It is in the context of the Davidic storyline that the emphasis in Proverbs becomes clear, "The Proverbs of Solomon, the Son of David, the King of Israel" (Prov 1:1). From the beginning, Solomon links Proverbs to the royal line of Israel and the messianic title "the Son of David." This reality should come as no surprise because Israel's leaders need wisdom to rule the kingdom in justice and to ensure its survival (1 Kings 3; Prov 29:14). In fact, Proverbs makes this very point (Prov 8:15-16). This emphasis is the wisdom through which readers should approach the text of Proverbs.

Proverbs is a book in which Solomon trains his "son" (the crown prince) in wisdom. The Bible defines Wisdom as obedience to the covenant (Deut 4:6; 6:1-9; 17:14-20), a wisdom that must be lived out in order to establish the Messianic kingdom.[9] The authors of Proverbs also wish to see this wisdom established in the youth of the nation through instruction.

When reading Proverbs, it is important to remember that the king embodies and represents the nation as a whole. If the king is wise, then the people will be wise. If the king is a fool, then the nation will walk in foolishness. The latter was the problem in Judges. There was no wise king so the people walked in the foolishness of their "own eyes." Proverbs understands that the king and the nation need wisdom for security and safety from their enemies. In the same way, every contemporary reader of Proverbs has a need to be ruled by the wisdom of the Messianic King, lest we be destroyed by our own foolishness. The king will produce the wisdom of Proverbs in his people, and that is why Solomon trains his sons, and the Spirit trains the reader through Proverbs

Examples of Solomon teaching his sons how to rule are found throughout the book. Again, in order for the dynasty to endure, the king had to be a man of the Law (Deut 17:14-20), so Solomon insists that his readers be devoted to "my law" (Prov 3:1; 4:2). Since the king was commanded to write a copy of the Law (Deut 17:18), he could call it "mine" while still referencing the Word of God. Obedience to the Law of God is how wisdom manifests itself.

Wisdom is living daily in faithfulness to the covenant of the Lord. God taught that the king must live in such a way to establish an enduring kingdom. If the crown prince breaks the covenant and walks in foolishness—for example, by falling for a foreign woman (1 Kings 11:1; Deut 17:17)—then it will lead to exile (Prov 2:16-22). If he walks in wisdom, however, then the kingdom will last forever. Thus, Proverbs 29:4 concludes, "The king will cause the land to endure by justice, but a man of bribes will overthrow it" (author's translation). Whether or not the king possesses the wisdom to do justice will determine whether the land and the kingdom will experience stability. An unjust judge will lead to the kingdom's disintegration and exile, but a just, wise king will lead to an eternal kingdom. "A king who judges the poor with truth, his throne will be established forever" (Proverbs 29:14, author's translation). This verse provides an accurate commentary on the Davidic dynasty. As the sons of David failed and the kingdom was lost in exile, the hope for a Greater David, or a Solomon-type king who actually would live out the wisdom of Proverbs began to grow.

Fulfillment in the New Testament

As New Testament Christians, we can see the fulfillment of this aforementioned expectation in Matthew 12 when one who is "greater than Solomon" arrives on the scene (12:42). Jesus of Nazareth is not only the wise king who keeps the wisdom of Proverbs, establishing his eternal kingdom, he also is the kingly sage who dispenses wisdom by teaching in "proverbs." The Septuagint refers to the proverbs as *paroimiai* (Prov 1:1) and *parabole* (Prov 1:6), which are the same words used in the New Testament to describe much of the teaching of Jesus (*paroimiai*—John 10:6; 16:25, 29; *parabole*—Matthew 13:3, 10, 13, 18, 24, 31, 33-36, 53; 21:33, 45; 22:1). When Jesus teaches, he teaches with proverbs as he dispenses the very wisdom that will order his kingdom.

For example, when Jesus taught about his kingdom in the Sermon on the Mount, he dealt with themes very similar to that of Proverbs.[10] First, the sermon—like Proverbs—presents two "ways" that lead to life or death (Matt 7:13-14; cf. Prov 2:1-15; 14:12). The citizen in Christ's Kingdom is the "wise man" who hears the words of the King-sage and does them, but the "fool" is the one who does not heed them and is destroyed by the storm (Matt 7:24-27; Prov 1:26-27). The wise who obey the sermon will "inherit the land," the same promise given to the wise in Proverbs (Matt 5:5; Prov 2:20-22). Second, the king's wisdom is based upon the Law. In the Sermon on the Mount, Jesus presents himself as the fulfillment of the Law and the Prophets (5:17-20). A King has finally arrived on the scene that both adheres to and accomplishes the Law (Matt 5:18; Deut 17). This King-sage dispenses his wisdom, as Solomon did before him, by teaching the Law (Matt 5:17-48).

Jesus did not discard the Law. Rather, he radicalized and internalized its application, which is one of the reasons why there are themes in the Law and Proverbs that are also a major focus in the Sermon on the Mount. Two examples are murder (Matt 5:21-22; cf. Exod 20:13; Prov 1:11) and adultery (Matt 5:27-30; cf. Exod 20:14; Prov 2:16-19; 5:1-23; 6:24-35), both of which lead to destruction.

The Sermon on the Mount and Proverbs have a similar ethic as well. Both command a love of enemies rather than retaliation (Matt 5:38-48; Prov 25:21). Additionally, the author of Proverbs observes nature in order to draw out principles of wisdom, which Jesus does similarly when he points his followers to the birds and the flowers as the reasons to trust in God's provision (Matt 6:25-34; Prov 30:18-33). The King-sage who is greater than Solomon teaches his followers what life in the kingdom should look like. He does so with the themes, language, and function of the Proverbs. The gospel writers present Jesus as the

King-sage who orders the long-awaited, wise, righteous, and eternal Davidic kingdom.

How to Preach Christ from Proverbs

The Sermon on the Mount is often discouraging to those who read it. After all, who can live up to its standard? The good news for those of us who are crushed by the weight of wisdom's standard and our inability to live up to it—whether it be the standard of Proverbs or the Sermon on the Mount—is that King Jesus himself is the one who lives out the life of the kingdom. *He* is the meek one who will inherit the whole earth. *He* is the one who loves his enemies and prays for those who nail him to the cross. *He* is the King who can produce the ethics of the kingdom in his followers. The only way to live out the wisdom of Proverbs (or the Sermon on the Mount) is through submission to the King in genuine faith.

When we preach Proverbs, therefore, we must expose our audience's failure to live up to the ethical standard it reveals, whether it be a refusal to forgive, a failure to speak up when they knew they should have, or a hundred of the other daily failures in our lives. As the standard of Proverbs reveals our shortcomings, Christ can then be presented as the wise King we all need to rule our foolish appetites that follow what our eyes tell us is true. We preach that Christ and Christ alone is the King-Sage who can produce this wisdom in his kingdom-citizens because he has already kept it perfectly.

The Second Feature: The Purpose of Proverbs is to Impart Wisdom

The purpose of Proverbs is to instruct the reader in wisdom, which is a wide and varied complex of ideas in Scripture, especially in the writings of Solomon, Agur, and Lemuel.

The Definition of Wisdom in Proverbs

In Proverbs, the father's (King Solomon) goal is to impart wisdom to his son (the crown prince). He uses the phrase "my son" over 15 times (1:8, 10, 15; 2:1; 3:1, 11, 21; 4:10, 20; 5:1, 20; 6:1, 3, 20; 7:1; etc.), and often starts his lectures by imploring his son to listen to his wise teachings. The father also wants to instruct the simple, the youth, and the wise in wisdom (1:4-6). Since the goal of the book is to impart wisdom, it raises an important question: "How does Solomon define wisdom?" A simple reading of Proverbs reveals that the father's understanding is multi-faceted. Solomon begins his work by using co-referential terms to describe what wisdom is.

> To know wisdom and instruction, to understand words of insight, to receive instruction in wise

dealing, in righteousness, justice, and equity; to give prudence to the simple, knowledge and discretion to the youth – Let the wise hear and increase in learning, and the one who understands obtain guidance, to understand a proverb and a saying, the words of the wise and their riddles (1:2-6).

While wisdom is equated with "instruction" in to the English Standard Version (1:2), a better translation may be "correction" or "discipline" (1:2).[11] Being wise requires a discipleship-type relationship in which individuals one can be warned, rebuked, or told when they are walking in the wrong direction. In order to have this kind of relationship, one must first have the ability to recognize in humility that he or she is not wise and submit to the counsel of another (i.e. a parent, a pastor, the community of faith, etc.). Ultimately, Christians must be able to submit to the authority of the Lord himself by submitting to the authoritative relationships he has placed in their lives (cf. Eph 6:1).

Wisdom is also "insight," or "understanding" (1:2). Understanding is knowledge that helps someone recognize what is happening around him or her. Additionally, wisdom is discernment or discretion (1:4), which is the ability to read people or a situation and make the right decision. The author of Proverbs desires to impart this skill to the youth and the gullible. The gullible are those who might readily embrace foolish advice, believing every word they are told. They are easily enticed, and typically persuaded by the very last words they hear. Solomon wants to give the gullible the ability to discern what is right or wrong concerning what they hear and see.

In addition to correction and insight, Proverbs also equates wisdom with the pursuit of guidance. Gaining wisdom is an education process. The wise obtain guidance (1:5) because they want to increase in wisdom. They not only need to grow in learning, but they also need to receive direction as well, which requires humility even for the wise. It's a humility that recognizes "I have not arrived yet." In other words, the humble desire to learn and to pursue wisdom. The humble recognize that an attitude of "I don't have all the answers" is essential to gaining true wisdom. One must have a humble desire for growth before he or she will receive counsel from another, see that counsel as wise, and put it into practice.

Through an examination of Solomon's opening words, it becomes clear that the point of Proverbs is to help readers understand the multi-faceted nature of wisdom so they can live wisely and make wise decisions. Through the inspiration of the Holy Spirit, Solomon has revealed to us that wisdom entails understanding, the correction of wrong thinking and living, discernment, the ability to read people and situations, and a humble pursuit of guidance from wise counselors.

Fulfillment in the New Testament

According to the New Testament, Jesus is the fulfillment of the wisdom of Proverbs because he is the "son" who grew in wisdom (Luke 2:40). Additionally, he pursued wisdom when he stayed behind in Jerusalem and spent time with the teachers "listening to them and asking them questions" (Luke 2:46). The text says that "all who heard him were amazed at his *understanding* and his answers" (emphasis mine; see also Prov 1:2). Luke ended the chapter by telling his readers that Jesus was a submissive son who obeyed his parents and that he "increased in wisdom and in stature and in favor with God and man" (Luke 2:51-52; see also Prov 3:4).

Not only is Jesus the son who grew in wisdom and understanding, he used that wisdom and understanding during his ministry to read people and situations expertly. He knew when people were testing him or attempting to trap him. He knew the motives behind the questions he was asked. In Matthew 22, the Pharisees plotted to "entangle him in his words" with regard to paying taxes to Caesar (22:15). Jesus, however, aware of the "malice" in their hearts answers, "Why put me to the test you hypocrites?" (22:18). When he answers them with a question about the inscription on the coin, the text says the Pharisees "marveled" (22:22). Jesus was, and is, the embodiment of the wisdom of Proverbs. He is the wise son.

How to Preach Christ

Therefore, when preaching passages such as Proverbs 26:4-5, the preacher should interpret the text with the example of Jesus as the wise son in mind.[12] Proverbs 26:4-5 reads, "Answer not a fool according to his folly, lest you be like him yourself. Answer a fool according to his folly, lest he be wise in his own eyes." This verse is not a collection of contradictory sayings. Rather, it teaches the reader that discernment is needed to read people or situations and to know when to respond. Proper application of this text requires that one discern the outcome of a particular situation. Will answering a fool help him, or will it simply be playing his game? One is likely to encounter both situations on a regular basis. Wisdom is the ability to assess which is which. Jesus amazed people with this ability. He knew when to stay silent because a reply would do no good. He also knew when to respond because he could read people and situations.

The New Testament provides many examples of Jesus' winsome application of Proverbs 26:4-5. In Matthew 15, the Pharisees challenged Jesus because his disciples were not following their perceived application of the law. Jesus, however rebukes them for their own violations of the Law (not honoring their fathers and mothers) in order to keep them from being wise in their own eyes (Matt 15:1-9). In Matthew 16, Peter foolishly rebukes Jesus concerning the cross, but Jesus answers him directly "Get behind me Satan" in order to correct his foolishness (Matt 16:23). Conversely, in Matthew 21:27, Jesus refused to play his opponents' game and did not answer them according to their foolishness.

Consequently, when we preach Proverbs 26:4-5, we need to teach our people that growth in Christ's likeness is much more than growth in our ability to avoid sin. Being conformed to the image of Christ also means growing in discernment. The maturing Christian should increasingly sense when a "friend" on Facebook just wants to argue, and therefore should choose not to engage him or her further. At the same time, the growing Christian will recognize increasingly when to speak up when the situation calls for an answer.

A lack of growth in this area reveals more than a lack of effort, it reveals an issue with Jesus that calls for repentance of sin and submission. The person who lacks discernment is not believing the gospel fully (2 Peter 1:9); idolatry is present and it prevents spiritual growth and maturity. The idol may be self-justification, which manifests itself in argumentativeness from a desire to be right. On the other hand, the idol may be self-approval, which manifests itself in a refusal to rebuke an erring brother or sister because of a desire to be liked by everyone. There may be another idol lurking behind one's failure to believe and apply the gospel, but there is always a heart issue that needs to be addressed. If you are in Christ, then you are the "son" who should be growing in wisdom, and that means growth in reading situations. Proverbs is all about imparting this kind of wisdom to you through Jesus Christ.

The Third Feature: Wisdom is the Knowledge of Good and Evil

There seems to be a popular opinion among some preachers that wisdom and foolishness are ethically neutral categories, that foolishness is just silliness and immaturity. Some have even concluded, "Well, foolishness is not exactly sin, but it's just not wise or helpful." Foolishness in Proverbs is more than merely silliness. Wisdom is more than the possession of a high intelligence quotient. Smart people can be fools. Contrary to popular opinion, there is a moral and ethical component to wisdom.

Solomon uses the words "righteousness" and "justice" (Prov 1:3) to describe wisdom. Wisdom is the ability to tell right from wrong in a given situation. In other words, wisdom and foolishness both have ethical components. An example from popular television illustrates the difference between wisdom in the world's eyes and wisdom as defined by Scripture. In the cartoon "The Simpsons," the character Bart is presented as a fool because of his shenanigans, whereas Maggie is perceived to be wise because she is smart and in control of the situation. From the viewpoint of Proverbs, however, Maggie is just as foolish as Bart because she fails to honor her father and treats him like a fool. A biblical worldview understands rebellion toward authority to be just as foolish, if not more so, than immaturity. Foolishness is the lack of discernment between good and evil. It is a sin to be a fool!

Old Testament Background

The Bible describes the connection between sin and folly in the Garden. There, God withheld the knowledge of good and evil from his people—Adam and Eve. He did not forbid the fruit of that tree as a random test to see whether or not Adam and Eve would obey him. Rather, he wanted them to depend on him and his Word for that knowledge. Adam and Eve, however, followed the foolishness "of their own eyes," revolted, and grasped for knowledge apart from God's Word because they thought it would make them "wise." Instead, they became fools (cf. Rom 1).

In spite of Adam's and Eve's failure, God again reveals the knowledge of good and evil to his people through his Word, the Law. Deuteronomy 4:6 teaches that Israel's wisdom before the surrounding nations is keeping the Law, so the Law--right and wrong—is tied directly to wisdom. Deuteronomy 6 commands parents to teach this knowledge to their kids as they go through life in order that they may stay long in the land (contra Adam and Eve, who were exiled from the Garden).

Deuteronomy 17 teaches that the king must be a man of the Law and learn to fear the Lord by keeping the Law in order for his dynasty to endure in the land. Solomon foolishly violated much of Deuteronomy 17. He returned to Egypt by marrying Pharaoh's daughter (1 Kings 3:1), he accumulated wives (1 Kings 11:1-3), and he accumulated money (1 Kings 10:14-29)—actions which lead to the ruin of his dynasty (Deut 17:16-17). Instead, Deuteronomy 17 instructs the wise king to copy the Law, to read it daily, and to learn to fear the Lord in order to establish his dynasty in the land (Josh 1:8; Psa. 1:2-3).

One finds repetition of the deuteronomic principle—that wisdom involves the knowledge of good and evil that is found in the Law (Deut 4:6)—in the book of Ezra. There, King Artaxerxes writes about "the Law of your God which is in your hand" (Ezra 7:14) and then subsequently refers to the Law as "the wisdom of your God which is in your hand" (7:25). It is the same principle revealed in Proverbs. In the end, wisdom is the knowledge of good and evil, which involves learning to view the world through the lens of Yahweh's covenant with Israel revealed in the law. Wisdom is the daily application of the law.

The Knowledge of Good and Evil in Proverbs

Proverbs reveals Solomon's obedience to the deuteronomic principles mentioned above. Solomon obeyed the commands of Deuteronomy 6 (everyone is to teach the Law to their children) and Deuteronomy 17 (the king was to be a man of the Law) by training his son to be a covenant-keeper.[13] Solomon refers to his teaching as "law" throughout the book. In fact, one of the reasons why Proverbs appears to be so "random" is because of the command in Deuteronomy 6 to teach your children when they get up, walk by the way, and lie down (i.e. all of life's activities). According to Deuteronomy 6, you teach your children as you go through life. How does one teach their kids? You do not teach your kids systematically by saying, "On Tuesday I will teach you about sex, on Wednesday finances, and on Thursday work ethic." No, in a given day you might tackle a hundred different topics by seizing opportunities in life as teachable moments, then working to apply a biblical worldview. Proverbs is a collection of seemingly disconnected teachings because the wise parent or leader must be equipped to deal with a variety of issues at any given moment. This emphasis on training children, which is so closely connected with Deuteronomy 6, and the connection with King Solomon (cf. Deut 17).

Proverbs repeatedly emphasizes that the key to wisdom is the internalization of the "law" of Solomon (Prov 2:1; 3:1, 3; 4:4; 6:21; 7:1, 3). Solomon used the language of Deuteronomy 6 when he instructed his readers to bind the teachings on their "neck" (3:1ff; Deut 6 commands that the Law be bound on your hands and as frontlets between your eyes). Proverbs 3:3 and 7:3 command the readers to write the law of Solomon—wisdom—on the tablet of their hearts.

The Ten Commandments were written on stone tablets (Exod 31:18) when they were given to the Israelites. The nation did not obey the commandments, however, because they could *not* obey them. The people did not have a "heart in them" that would cause them to fear Yahweh and keep his commands (Deut 5:29). An inner transformation had to take place called "circumcision of the heart" (Deut 10:16). Israel's problem was that Yahweh had not given them such a heart (Deut 29:3). Yet, Yahweh promised that a day was coming when he would circumcise their hearts himself so they could obey him (Deut 30:6). In fact, Deuteronomy 4 functions as an eschatological warning where it ominously predicts what Israel's history will be: disobedience to the law, exile, and then redemption when they would be transformed from the inside-out, which would enable them to keep the Law. Moses wrote that this transformation would happen in the "latter days" (Deut 4:25-30).

This promise is repeated in Ezekiel's prophecy of a new heart (Ezek 36:26) and Jeremiah's prophecy of the New Covenant: "'But this is the covenant I will make with the house of Israel after those days,' says the Lord 'I will put my law in their minds, and write it on their hearts'" (Jer 31:33). Proverbs joins the promises of Deuteronomy and the prophets together by saying the Law will be written on the tablet (Old Covenant) of your heart (New Covenant; Prov 3:3; 7:3). In order to walk in the wisdom of Proverbs, an inner transformation needs to take place. Proverbs does not teach that wisdom is found in simple behavior modification nor does it imply any kind of works based righteousness.

Regeneration is necessary to walk in wisdom. One must be born again because "wise living" is a matter of the heart. The "fool" in Proverbs literally "lacks a heart" (Prov 6:32; 7:7; 9:4; 10:13; 11:12; 12:11; 17:18; 24:30; see also Deut 5:29). Woman Wisdom and Woman Folly seek the affection of the one who lacks heart (9:4, 16). Additionally, Proverbs teaches that the adulterer is someone who lacks a heart (Prov 6:32; 7:7), that the lazy fool lacks a heart, and finally that the one who lacks a heart will die (10:21). The wise person, however, who listens to wisdom "gains" a heart (15:32; see also Ezek 36:26). Not only must a person have the Law written on his or her heart to obey, he or she must also receive the Spirit (Prov 1:23). Wisdom requires regeneration.

Fulfillment in the New Testament

Proverbs points to Jesus with its ethical demands and repeated calls for inward transformation. The authors of Proverbs teach this transformation not only helps one *discern* good from evil, but also provides the power to *walk* in righteousness as opposed to evil (Prov 2:12). This language is the language of regeneration, of new birth. The New Testament reveals that regeneration happens only by the gospel of Jesus Christ. His blood was shed to inaugurate the New Covenant. He rose and ascended that we might receive his gift of the Holy Spirit. In order to be transformed, one must believe the gospel, receiving the transforming gift of life that is Jesus Christ.

Proverbs also points to Jesus with its repeated emphasis on obedience to the law. Jesus is the fulfillment of the Law. He is the Son of Solomon who fulfills the wisdom of Proverbs perfectly. He is the Messiah of Isaiah 11 who embodies the wisdom of Proverbs. He is the one who grows in wisdom and stature and favor with God and man (Lk 2:50-52; Prov 3:4). He is the covenant-keeping King who hears and obeys the call of Deuteronomy 6 and 17. Jesus perfectly obeyed Deuteronomy 4:6. He was the wise person who kept the Law. All of the "laws" of Proverbs that threaten death to those who break them were obeyed by Jesus (Prov 1:8-19; 2:12-22; etc.).

Even though Jesus perfectly kept the covenant, he also took on the curses that covenant-breakers deserved by going into the chambers of Sheol for them (Pro 7:27). He died on the cross in the place of fools who rejected the wisdom of Proverbs, who walked in a path that lead to death and judgment. He took the penalty that everyone deserves. When fools recognize their foolishness, confess it to the Lord, and turn from it in faith towards Jesus, they will receive forgiveness and the righteousness of Jesus Christ. His perfectly wise obedience to the Law is credited to the account of the believer in addition to new birth, and the gradual process of transformation by the Spirit that conforms believers into the wise image of Jesus.

How to Preach Christ from Proverbs

Keeping two imperatives in mind when preparing sermons from Proverbs will help you point your audience to Christ. First, avoid moralism. Preach for heart change rather than behavior modification. Second, as you proclaim the ethical and behavioral standards of Proverbs, be sure to remind your listener that Christ is the only one that has met that standard. Our need is to trust him for our right standing before God, which frees us to obey the law, or in this case, the Proverbs.

Avoid moralism. Our nature determines how we walk. It must be changed by the gospel for us to walk in wisdom. Proverbs 4:23 reminds us that everything in our lives—our words, our actions, and the course of our lives—flows from our heart. Our hearts are impure (Prov 20:9), so we walk in a way that seems right but ends in destruction (Prov 14:12). According to the Proverbs, the Law of wisdom must be written on your heart in order for inward transformation to take place. Consequently, merely preaching to modify behavior does not produce transformation. Such an approach only deals with a symptom of the problem, not the source of the problem. Our hearts are the central command centers of our lives, so transformational preaching must deal with the heart before behavior. If our sermons address behavior, but not the heart which produces said behavior, then the sin in the heart will manifest itself in another way in the lives of our people.

For example, when counseling someone who is addicted to pornography, you can modify their behavior by putting blocking software on their computer. That is a helpful, and warranted approach. The lust in the person's heart, however, still exists and will find another way to express itself if not confronted by the gospel and the Spirit of Christ. The addict might find other avenues to view pornography, he might lust after the women in his office, or he may just focus on the images he remembers from his previous encounters. The root of the problem has not been dealt with, only the fruit. Proverbs calls us to deal with foolishness and sin at the heart level in order to see lasting change. To avoid moralistic preaching, you must address the motives and desires of the heart that manifest themselves in particular sin, then demonstrate how the gospel addresses those motives.

Present Christ as the Law's fulfillment. Second, when preaching Proverbs, remind your audience that Jesus is the only one that has ever met the moral and ethical standard the book reveals. In this respect, preaching Proverbs will be very much like preaching Jesus from the Law. Many of the messages will follow a similar pattern. First, present wisdom's standard. Do not lie, obey your parents, do not be lazy, do not fall into adultery, or do not be bitter toward those who have wronged you. Second, show your audience how they have fallen short of that standard. We all have lied, have talked back to our parents, been lazy, lusted after others in our hearts, or remained angry with someone who wronged us, etc. Third, explain that Jesus lived his life without sin and never failed in any of the aforementioned areas. No deceit was found in his mouth. He was subject in everything to Mary and Joseph. He finished all of the work the Father gave him to do. He never fell into sexual sin, and he forgave those who wronged him. Fourth, proclaim the fact that Jesus bore the punishment and death that fools deserved when he died on the cross so that fools like us could be forgiven, made new, and given eternal life. Finally, teach your audience that through the indwelling Word and Spirit of Christ, God conforms his children into the wise image of Jesus so that they can begin to live out the wisdom of Proverbs in their daily lives. Jesus is wisdom *for us*, as well as righteousness and sanctification (1 Cor 1:30, emphasis mine). Living faith in Jesus is what produces wisdom in us and sanctifies us to grow in righteousness. Indeed, Proverbs reveals our folly and points us to Jesus, the Wisdom of God, who can rescue us from our foolishness and indeed make us wise for salvation (2 Tim 3:15).

The Fourth Feature: The Fear of the Lord is the Key Component to Wisdom

The musical group D. H. T. sang "Listen to your heart; there's nothing else you can do!" It is the cry of a generation that screams, "Follow your heart, and you can't go wrong!" From Disney movies to "The Bachelor," we are told to follow our hearts in order to make the best decisions for our lives. Whom should I date? Whom should I marry? Should I stay married? What career path should I choose? To answer such questions, the culture asks, "What does your heart tell you?" Even "Christian" counsel often seems to be a mixture of Bible verses coupled with "follow your heart." Such counsel is foolish. Left to ourselves, we choose wrongly because we have sinful hearts. We do not see the world properly, so we make decisions that ruin our lives. Proverbs tells us that human wisdom is foolish, so we need to look to God and his Word for true wisdom. The fear of the Lord is the beginning or key component of wisdom (Prov 1:7).

Old Testament Background

Because of our inherent sin nature, all human beings are programmed to reject the voice of God and listen to the wrong voice—usually our own! This problem has existed since the Adam's and Eve's failure in the Garden.

In fact, the early chapters of Genesis are presented in wisdom language.[14] The Lord warned the man to not eat from the tree of the knowledge of good and evil because He was teaching humanity to depend on God and his Word for knowledge. We are not to determine ethics for ourselves. We are not the arbiters of what is good and what is evil. God is. We are to rely on God for this knowledge instead of asserting our autonomy.

As has been previously discussed in this chapter, the voice of the "crafty" (Gen 3:1; Prov 12:23) serpent deceived Eve into pursuing what she thought would make her wise (Gen 3:6). Foolishness is pursuing what your eyes say is right instead of listening to the Word of God (cf. Prov 3:5-7). She rejected God's word, listened to the serpent's word, and chose what her eyes told her was wise. So did Adam. Trusting yourself and listening to Satan go hand-in-hand. Eve sought wisdom and knowledge apart from God. Her decision brought destruction and led to death and the downfall of humanity.

Eve tried to become the arbiter of what was good and evil instead of allowing God's Word to determine those realities. Humanity has been making the same mistake ever since. All of us have chosen to disobey the Word. We have chosen the wisdom of the world over the wisdom of God. As a result, we now live in a culture that is the fruit of Adam's and Eve's sin in the Garden. We believe we are entitled to determine right and wrong for ourselves. We allow our culture to determine our ethics! We think we can define marriage for ourselves, that we can determine proper sexual ethics for ourselves, that we can decipher what is tolerant and intolerant, and much more. Contemporary culture is not new. Humanity has been this way since the fall of Adam and Eve.

The Fear of the Lord in Proverbs

According to Proverbs, the very autonomy that Adam and Eve pursued, that you and I pursue, is foolishness. Folly is listening to the voice of the serpent rather than the Word of God.[15] Folly is following what is "right in our own eyes" rather than what God has said is right (Prov 3:5-7; 30:5-6). On the other hand, wisdom is found in the fear of the Lord. There is a contrast between human wisdom—which is foolishness—and godly wisdom. True wisdom comes from the mouth of God (Prov 2:6) and leads to life. The way that seems right to a man ends in death (Prov 14:12). Following our own sinful hearts is not only foolish, it is destructive. "Whoever trusts in his own heart is a fool, but he who walks in wisdom will be delivered" (Proverbs 28:26, author's translation). It is wrong to follow our hearts because our hearts are sinful. Proverbs 20:9 asks, "Who can say, 'I have made my heart pure; I am clean from my sin'?" The expected answer is, "no one!" Because of our sinful and impure condition, we do not choose rightly. We do not see things clearly. Following our hearts is deadly because we will not be "delivered" (i.e. saved). Instead, we are to follow godly wisdom.

There are things that are wise to God that are foolishness to men, and there are things that are foolishness to God that we think are wise (1 Cor 1). Our logic is contaminated by sin. Our hearts are so blind, we cannot even see our own folly. God's wisdom clashes with the wisdom of the world. The world says, "If you want to be rich, then you need to be stingy and keep things for yourself." Godly wisdom, however says, "One gives freely, yet grows all the richer; another withholds what he should give, and only suffers want" (Prov 11:24). The world says, "Money will make you happy, so get as much as you can." Godly wisdom counters, "Whoever trusts in his riches will fall" (Prov 11:28) and "the righteous has enough to satisfy his appetite" (Prov 13:25). Godly wisdom calls us to be content with what we have!

The world says, "If you want to get ahead in life, then you need to promote yourself." God says, "Let another praise you and not your own mouth" (Prov 27:2). The world says, "Be friends with your kids. Don't discipline or say 'no' to them." God says, "He who loves his son is diligent to discipline him" (Prov 13:24). Worldly wisdom says, "Go along to get along. Don't jeopardize friendships by having difficult conversations; it's not your business anyways." But, godly wisdom says, "Better an open rebuke than hidden love" (Prov 27:5).

Some of the aforementioned worldly sayings are obviously foolish. Others, however, are not so obvious. Our big problem is not a lack of information, but rather a failure see the world properly because of our heart condition. That problem is compounded by the fact that we are oblivious to our condition apart from the gift of God's grace! We are wise in our own eyes, which Proverbs teaches is the epitome of foolishness (Prov 21:2). Foolishness is a lot like colorblindness, with which I suffer. At my house, one of our girls' favorite games is to hold up items and ask daddy, "What color is this?" while giggling uncontrollably because I can't answer! I cannot see colors rightly—they look different to me than most people. That is how Proverbs describes foolishness. The fool is unable to see the world the way it really is.

"There is a way that seems right to a man but in the end it leads to death" (Prov 14:12; 16:25). What seems like the right course to fools in Proverbs, actually leads to ruin and death because they do not see things clearly. Left to ourselves, we will choose the wrong way because we are self-deceived. "The way of a fool is right in his own eyes, but a wise man listens to advice" (Prov 12:15).

It is foolish to think our way is always right and not to listen to godly counsel in our lives, whether it comes from a parent, a pastor, or a godly friend. We need to be warned against trusting ourselves and admonished to trust the Lord. "Trust in the Lord with all your heart, and do not lean on your own understanding" (Prov 3:5). These options are two sides of the same coin: trust God, not yourself. "Be not wise in your own eyes" (Prov 3:7). Foolishness is thinking that we are wise; it is produced by and reveals a lack of humility. Instead, we need to trust God and his Word.

The message "trust God, not yourself" is the simplified message of Proverbs. Wisdom is found in God. He made the world; he knows how it works. This message is what Solomon implies when he writes that the fear of the Lord is the key component to wisdom (Prov 1:7; 9:10; etc.). There are two components to gaining wisdom: trusting God and trusting his Word. The fear of God, of which Solomon speaks, is reverent awe and dependence upon God that leads to obedience.

To obey the primary message of Proverbs (3:5) requires humility, which is almost synonymous in Proverbs with the fear of the Lord (Prov 15:31-33). The first step to wisdom is to realize that we are not wise. In order to have knowledge, we must first recognize that we do not know everything and we are not always right. Wisdom begins by being humble enough to admit this truth, then submitting to God and his wise counsel. On the other hand, pride is the essence of foolishness. "When pride comes, then comes disgrace, but with the humble is wisdom" (Prov 11:2). Humility is essential for wisdom. Even those who *are* wise still need counsel and correction (Prov 9:9).

The fear of God and the knowledge of God are parallel concepts (Prov 2:5). The bottom line is that a personal relationship with God is the key to wisdom. We fear him because He is the one who gives wisdom. It comes from his mouth. It is the Word of God (Prov 2:6; Prov 30:5-6). In order to fear God and be wise, we must go to his Word and submit to its authority for our lives.

Reverent awe of the Lord is the key to wisdom (Prov 1:7; 1:29; 2:5; 8:13; 9:10; 10:27; 14:26-27; 15:16, 33; 16:6; 19:23; 22:4; 23:17). Once we have a right relationship with God, then we can have a right relationship with our neighbors and the world around us. Our vertical relationship with God must be right. Then our horizontal relationships will be right. Proverbs calls us to a return to the edenic paradise of harmony with God, others, and the world through covenant submission to the Lord and his Word. That is the only path to walk if one wants to navigate successfully through life.

An example of this approach to understanding of wisdom plays itself out in the warnings against adultery scattered throughout Proverbs (chapters 2, 5, 6, and 7). Proverbs 2 teaches that a man must have a right relationship with the Lord to be shielded from adultery (Prov 2:5-19). Proverbs 5 teaches that a man must have a right relationship with his wife to avoid adultery. The combination of these proverbs reveals the connection that exists between our vertical relationship with God and our horizontal relationships with others, a concept seen throughout the book. Solomon knew this truth well because his horizontal relationships with foreign women destroyed his vertical relationship with God (1 Kings 11).

Wisdom is only found through a covenant relationship with the Lord by faith. It is found in trusting the Lord and the design laid out in his Word with all our heart because we know he is good and wants the best for us. Proverbs calls us to submit to the Lord through his Word in every area of our lives: morality, friendships, family, money, job, tongue, and more. The book teaches that every day, seemingly amoral decisions are decisions about which the Lord cares. There is no secular and sacred divide according to Proverbs. Every area of our life is spiritual in nature. God is concerned with what seems to be routine, or even mundane, to us. God is concerned about such decisions because they reveal whether or not we fear him. How we eat dinner, discipline our children, and work our job, all indicate whether or not we fear the Lord. Every nook and cranny of our life is to be governed by God.   Intelligence is not an indicator of wisdom because the highly intelligent can live lives that are not submitted to God.

Trusting God and his Word brings life. "Blessed is the one who fears the Lord always, but whoever hardens his heart will fall into calamity" (Prov 28:14). There is blessing for those who fear the Lord, disaster for those who reject him. Trusting the Lord prolongs life, whereas folly can ruin life or lead to a premature death. Trusting the Lord has positive consequences for the family because it gives our children a refuge (Prov 14:26). Trusting the Lord prevents anxiety because it allows us to be satisfied in the Lord (Prov 19:23). Trusting the Lord leads to a good reputation, joy in life now, and eternal life in the age to come.

God's wisdom is often mediated through human agents like parents, counselors, or friends according to Proverbs. Foolishness is revealed by a refusal to submit to these agents because it reveals that one does not think they need counsel. Wisdom involves submitting to godly counsel that is consistent with God's Word.

Fulfillment in the New Testament

Adam and Eve, and by extension every one of us, rejected God's Word in the Garden, followed what our eyes told us was true, and now think we are wise when we are really fools. We do not see the world as it really is. There is hope, however. The New Testament presents one man who did not give in to temptation when he was in a garden. He said, "Not what I want but what you want," and he went to the cross. 1 Corinthians 1 tells us that Christ's obedience to the point of death is foolishness to the world, but it's the wisdom of God. If we are going to be wise in God's eyes, it will mean looking foolish in the eyes of the world because we embrace the gospel. If we are going to be wise, it means humble submission to the one who is God's wisdom and sanctification for us. We must fear Jesus to walk in wisdom.

Wisdom starts with a recognition of our own ignorance, which leads us to turn to one who is wise, Jesus Christ! In Proverbs 30:1-6, Agur acknowledges that he is not wise and that wisdom lies in heaven with God and with *his son* who has ascended and descended (Prov 30:4; emphasis mine). No one has gone up to God to get wisdom, so unless God reveals wisdom to us we have no hope of receiving it. The good news of the gospel is that God *has* revealed wisdom to us in his Word (Prov 30:5-6). That Word is more than a collection of pages in a book; it is flesh and bones (John 1:1). One can only become wise if he or she submits to the Son and is shaped by the Word. The Bible is sufficient to shape our thinking; we do not need to add to it (Prov 30:5-6). If we do not submit to Jesus through the Word, we will not view the world properly.

How to Preach Christ

Preaching Jesus from Proverbs means exhorting others to faith in our covenant Lord as the only means to walk in wisdom. Wisdom is only possible by faith in Jesus because by faith in Jesus estranged sinners (fools) are brought into a covenant relationship with God, which leads to right relationship with the world around them (Eph 2; faith in Christ reconciles sinners to God and to each other). We see this approach confirmed in Proverbs with teaching on issues such as bitterness and revenge. Worldly wisdom, or the flesh, says, "Hold on to a grudge." Proverbs teaches us not only to forgive, but gives the reason why we should forgive. We forgive because we are waiting on the Lord in full trust (Prov 20:22). After all, Jesus did not lash out when he was treated wrongly because he entrusted himself to the one who judges justly (1 Peter 2:23). Such forgiveness is often foolishness in the eyes of the world. It is wisdom, however, in the eyes of

God. So preach submission to Christ, which leads to wise living in the world.

The Fifth Feature: Wisdom is a Matter of Life and Death

The choice between wisdom and foolishness impacts more than our daily lives. This choice also has tremendous impact on our future—including eternity. Choosing wisdom above foolishness is a matter of life and death.

Old Testament Background

In Scripture, God consistently sets life and death before his people and says, "Choose!" He did so in Eden with the Tree of the Knowledge of Good and Evil. He did so in Deuteronomy 30 with the giving of the Law. He does the same in the wisdom literature, where sets before the reader wisdom that leads to life and foolishness that leads to death and says, "Choose!"

Life and Death in Proverbs

There are consequences for foolishness and rewards for wisdom in Proverbs; you reap what you sow. Wisdom leads to abundant and eternal life, whereas foolishness leads to ruin in this life and death in the life to come. Proverbs presents life and death as either immediate or future consequences. For example, life in Proverbs can refer to longer life (3:2), a better life (3:4), a great reputation (22:1), wealth (3:10), peace of mind (3:21-26), or eternal life (12:28). Death can refer to shame (5:14), premature death (5:5), loss of possessions (5:10), or exile (2:22). The immediate consequences like a great reputation or shame are a foretaste of ultimate consequences— eternal life in the land (New Heavens and New Earth) or the death of permanent exile under God's judgment.

The curse of death has reigned since the foolish decision of the first humans to follow what was right in their own eyes rather than believe God's Word. That rebellion cut us off from the Tree of Life and made it certain that we would return to the dust from which we were created (Gen 3:19), which coincides with what Proverbs 2:19 teaches: foolishness is the path to death where there is no hope of a return to the path of life.

Proverbs, however, also holds out hope that the curse of death can be overcome. "Treasures gained by wickedness do not profit, but righteousness *delivers from death*" (Prov 10:2, emphasis mine; see also 11:4). The path of righteousness is the way to escape death (Prov 12:28). "The path of life leads upward for the prudent, that he may turn away from Sheol beneath" (Prov 15:24). So, the path of wisdom leads away from death toward eternal life. The wisdom of God grants access to the Tree of Life (Prov 3:18).

A proper eschatological framework provides the key to understanding the consequences and rewards spoken of in Proverbs. Sometimes the rewards and retribution are granted immediately. At other times the results of our choices are delayed. Regardless of the *timing* of the consequences of our choices, their certainty is unquestioned in Proverbs. The temporary consequences we experience for our wise or foolish choices are merely a foretaste of the final outcomes. Consequently, being a fool will wreck your life now and forever, whereas being wise will bring you an abundant and eternal life that escapes the curse of death.

Preaching Christ as the Fulfillment of the Promises and Warnings of Proverbs

The preacher must be clear that the promises and consequences spoken of in Proverbs are fulfilled in Jesus, ultimately. *He* is the one who walked the path of righteous wisdom and thereby gained victory over death. On the one hand, Sheol is seen as an irresistible force and irreversible fate for the fool in Proverbs (1:12; 5:5; 7:27; 9:18; *et al*). The wages of foolishness is death with no possibility of return (Prov 2:16-18). On the other hand, wisdom is presented as the way to escape death. The gospel story is that Jesus went into Sheol because of our foolishness, then was delivered by the Father because he was blameless. Death could not hold or stop him because the righteous one—the wise one—was raised from Sheol. Resurrection life is available in him, but apart from him an irreversible grave awaits us, which is perfectly consistent with Proverbs 12:28, "In the path of righteousness is life, and in its pathway there is no death."

Apart from the gospel, that verse is not good news, because we have all sinned and fallen short of God's path of righteousness (Rom 3:23). If we are united with Christ by faith, however, there is immortality. Our only hope as sinners is to be found in the wise, righteous Son. As we trust him by faith, the Father counts us righteous before him and we will be delivered from death. If we stand before the Judge on our own merit we will perish because of our foolishness.

Chapter 3

Five More Christ-Centered Features in Proverbs

One of the main obstacles to our people becoming wise is the wrong notion – often communicated from our pulpits – that wisdom is simply about learning enough facts. We often imply with our preaching that wisdom is learning three steps to a better marriage, five tips to better finances, and four lessons for better parenting. Yet, Proverbs teaches us that Wisdom is a person that we can know, and that by virtue of knowing this person we actually are made wise! Proverbs also teaches that the world was created by means of wisdom, and therefore the world works in a certain way. Wisdom is the effort to discern that pattern and live your life by it, and even if the pattern does not work out immediately, it will work out ultimately. Wisdom is also a path or a way that you walk. Ultimately, the Bible reveals to us that the "way" and pattern of wisdom are a man: Jesus of Nazareth.

The Sixth Feature:
Wisdom is a Person

Unfortunately, too many Christians approach the book of Proverbs as if it were an Israelite version of Dear Abby that gives us tips for how to live a better life.[16] According to Proverbs, however, wisdom is not a set of ideas. Wisdom is a person. That is the point of Proverbs 1-9 as well as the interpretive key to understand the entire book. The message of the book boils down to one question: "With whom will you be in a relationship?" This is the fundamental question of chapters 1-9 that must be answered for the son to walk in the wisdom of the book (chapters 10-31). There are rivals competing for the son's attention and affection. Yes, some of them are physical rivals to the father like the immoral woman (2:16-19; 5:1-23; 7:1-27) and the gang of peers (1:10-19), but standing behind them is a spiritual rival, Woman Folly (9:13-18). As we will see, Folly refers to idols that are competing with Yahweh for the son's devotion.[17] So,

Proverbs 1-9 drives the son to choose between Wisdom and Folly, between Yahweh and idols. As the New Testament shows, Proverbs ultimately points us to a choice between Jesus and Satan.

Proverbs teaches that vertical and horizontal relationships are related to one another. How individuals respond to the physical rivals for wisdom reveals whom they are following spiritually (and vice versa). Those who listen and submit to the Father are revealed to have a right relationship with Wisdom (God; Eph 6:1). Those who commit adultery with the foreign woman, however, are revealed to be chasing after Folly (idols; ultimately Satan). Again, Solomon knows the consequences of ignoring God's wisdom in this instance firsthand. He failed when foreign women pulled his heart away from Yahweh to idols.

The "father" of Proverbs wants his son to choose Wisdom (God) over Folly (idols), so that he will walk in wisdom and avoid destruction. The context is similar to the Garden and is similar today. Will we choose Satan's voice over God's Word? If our vertical relationship is wrong, everything will be wrong. We will be unable to love our neighbor or navigate our way through the world. In Proverbs, Solomon is an evangelist exhorting his son to choose a relationship with Wisdom!

The Personification of Wisdom in Proverbs

In order to strengthen his exhortation, Solomon personifies his teaching on wisdom as an attractive woman. Personification occurs when an abstract idea is presented as a person or creature in order to grab attention or clarify a point. Modern examples of personification are phrases like "opportunity knocked" or "Lady Justice is blind." In Proverbs, Wisdom is presented as a person one must embrace in order to walk the wise path in daily life. If one would be wise at work, in the use of his or her tongue, or in his or her stewardship, then he or she has to know Woman Wisdom intimately.

Proverbs personifies Wisdom as a woman for two reasons. First, the Hebrew noun for wisdom (*hokma*) is feminine. When one uses personification in Hebrew the symbol assumes the gender of the noun. Second, the father knows what will entice his young son. Young men are drawn to attractive women.

Solomon progressively develops his personification of wisdom throughout the first nine chapters. In 1:20-33, Wisdom is a street preacher who pleads with the young man to repent. If he does, she will pour out the Spirit on him. If he refuses, however, his life will be ruined in certain judgment because he did not fear the Lord. Wisdom and Yahweh are shown to be connected in this passage. Refusing Wisdom is described as refusing to fear the Lord (Prov 1:25, 29). Wisdom threatens death to those who reject her and safety to those who embrace her.

In Proverbs 2, Wisdom can save the reader from the foreign woman, who also will become a major character in the book. She is the repeated subject of the father's warnings. The foreign woman is Solomon's competitor for the son's attention because her smooth words mimic his (2:16). Solomon warns his son that he will fall into sexual sin if he falls for her flattery. The foreign woman is later personified as Woman Folly (chapter 9), yet another rival to Wisdom.

Folly is described in the same way as the foreign woman. They both flatter and they both use smooth speech to lure their prey to death and the grave (5:3; 7:14-21; 9:13-17; 2:18; 7:27; 9:18). If the son embraces the foreign woman, then it reveals that he has rejected the father, Wisdom, and ultimately the Lord. Just as the Scriptures consistently reveal elsewhere, sexual sin and spiritual idolatry are tied together. Adultery is a distortion of the most intimate human relationship God has given us. It leads to the distortion of our most intimate spiritual relationship as well (1 Cor 6:12-20). This teaching underscores the primary message of Proverbs 1-9: if our horizontal relationships are off, then our vertical one will be as well (and vice versa). If Solomon's son falls for the foreign woman in Proverbs 2, it reveals that he is not in right relation with the Lord and will be led away from him as a result. Solomon exhorts his son to embrace Lady Wisdom who will rescue him from his folly.

In chapter 3, the father exhorts the son to get Wisdom because nothing he desires can compare with her. Wisdom is the pearl of great price worth selling all that he has in order to possess. In chapter 4, Solomon reveals that his father, David, also exhorted him to embrace Wisdom. Chapters 5-7 describe the rival to the father and Wisdom—the immoral, foreign woman. She is a real adulteress, hunting down the son as if he were her prey. Woman Folly stands behind the foreign woman (9:13-18; cf. Satan who is the roaring lion seeking to devour us). The antidote given in chapter 7, according to the father, is to marry Wisdom. He says that the son should say to Wisdom, "You are my sister," an ancient idiom which was a term of endearment for a beloved bride (cf. Song of Songs 4:9-5:2). One must be in a one-flesh union with Wisdom to be wise and to avoid the foreign woman who brings destruction!

Thus far, the personal dimension of Wisdom in Proverbs seems to be a literary device that represents the teachings of wisdom. The personification of Wisdom is an alternative to the gang of fools and the immoral woman. Proverbs 8, however, elevates the personification by showing it to be from God and more than a collection of sayings. Wisdom was there in the beginning (8:22), before the depths were brought forth (8:24), before the mountains (8:25), and before the Lord gave the sea its limits (8:29). Not only did Wisdom exist prior to the Creation, but Wisdom assisted the Lord *in* creation. She says, "I was beside him, like a master workman" (8:30). These are claims that Solomon could not make for himself or his teaching because it is the wisdom of God that is being described. The Lord created the world by means of wisdom and knowledge (3:19-20).

Proverbs 9 is the culmination of all that precedes the chapter and an interpretive hinge for everything that follows. In this chapter, the father presents Wisdom one final time in order to get his son (and the reader) to make a decision for her before discussing wisdom proper in chapters 10-31. Whether or not the son can follow the wisdom laid out in the rest of the book will be determined by his choice. Both Wisdom and Folly hold a marriage feast in their palaces and invite the son to attend (9:1-6, 13-18). The descriptions of their houses and their location begin to reveal the identities of these two personas. Their homes are at the highest point of the city which is a place reserved for temples. Deities dwell in temples. Proverbs 8 has already shown that Wisdom is God's Wisdom—it ultimately represents Yahweh himself.[18] Idols also have their temples at the highest place of the city, which is where Folly lives, so she ultimately represents idols.[19] Choosing Wisdom will lead to life; choosing Folly will lead to death. In this chapter, Solomon is urging his son to make a faith decision for Wisdom (Yahweh) instead of Folly (idols).

This decision is crucial because the son must have a relationship with Wisdom in order to walk in the wisdom that follows chapter nine. Conversely, whether or not he is walking in the wisdom of Proverbs reveals if he's following after Wisdom or Folly. For example, if he gives into the peer pressure of the gang of fools, the seduction of the foreign woman, if he can't control his tongue, or if he is lazy, his actions will reveal idolatry in his life. On the other hand, if he avoids the gang of fools, if he remains pure, if he obeys his father, if he has a good work ethic, and if he has control over his mouth, then it shows he's embraced Wisdom. This contrast is how Solomon wants the reader to understand the principles in the book. One must have a *relationship* with Wisdom in order to follow wisdom. If one is not living out the precepts of wisdom revealed in Proverbs it is because he or she is not following Wisdom—Jesus Christ.

Fulfillment in the New Testament

We are able to see the relationship between the person of Wisdom and wisdom more clearly than first readers of Proverbs because we read it in light of Jesus Christ, who is the perfect embodiment of Wisdom. He fulfills what Proverbs says about this figure called Wisdom. Additionally, Jesus clearly identifies himself as the fulfillment of "Woman Wisdom" (Matt 11:19; Luke 7:35). We now know that Jesus is the Wisdom of God for us (1 Cor 1:24, 30; Prov 8) and that "all the treasures of wisdom and knowledge" are hidden in him (Col 2:3). Proverbs confirms this truth for us. Wisdom does not reside with foolish humanity, but with God. Wisdom is God's Son who both ascended and descended; he is God's Word (Prov 30:4-6). This conclusion is sustained by John 1, Colossians 1, and Hebrews 1, which all present Jesus as the pre-existent Son who created and ordered the world.

The follies of our lives reveal our need of Jesus. If we want wise lives, then we must have a relationship with Christ, the embodiment of wisdom.

How to Preach Christ

The fact that Jesus is Wisdom and a relationship with him is the key to wise living shows how the preacher is to proclaim the gospel from these sections of Proverbs. Think of the sheer number of foolish decisions we make in this life, of hurtful words spoken, of the times we said more than we should have, or of times we spoke quickly without thinking. Think of the times we failed to listen to others, the times we lied, the times we spread gossip, or the times we were prideful of ourselves, our position, or our accomplishments. These failures are but a small portion of the list of ways in which we fail to measure up to the way of wisdom revealed in Proverbs. Trying to follow wisdom when confronted with our failures is depressing. We can see the warnings of consequences about to bear fruit in our lives.

But what if wisdom was more than a concept or a set of ideas you had to learn? What if wisdom was a person you could know and with whom you could have a relationship? A person who spoke to you? Whom you could follow? And what if by virtue of knowing that person and loving that person, that person could actually make you wise? The Good News of the gospel is that Wisdom is a person, and his name is Jesus. Knowing him personally will make you wise.[20] Through Jesus, you can be reconciled to God, to other people, and to the world around you. By knowing Jesus and being made like him you will be empowered to walk in the proverbial wisdom of chapters 10-31. You will be conformed to his wise image!

Here is how this truth should be presented when preaching Proverbs. Since Wisdom (Jesus) and Folly

(Idols or Satan) are rivals competing for our faith, the choice we make between Jesus and idols will determine whether we walk the path of wisdom or foolishness. The only way we can heed the practical advice in Proverbs 10-31 is if Proverbs 1-9 has led us into a personal relationship with the Wisdom of God who is Jesus Christ. Whether or not we are walking in wisdom—finishing our tasks on time, obeying our parents, managing our finances properly, listening to advice we need to hear, and more—reveals where we are with Jesus. So, as you preach the Proverbs to your people (and yourself) and see a failure to control the tongue, laziness, grudges and a lack of forgiveness, or a hundred other very practical things, it that reveals that a problem in their (or our) relationship with Jesus. Walking in the way of wisdom reveals we are following Christ. A failure to do so reveals we are idolaters.

Proverbs 10:1 teaches, "A wise son makes a glad father, but a foolish son is a sorrow to his mother." This verse should be understood to imply that being a foolish child who shames his or her parents is a form of idolatry. Being a being a wise son or daughter who brings them joy reveals a life that follows Christ. Idols of self-centeredness and pride can keep us from submitting to parental authority, but Jesus demonstrated he was the Wisdom of God when he submitted in all things to his parents (Luke 2:51) and honored them by taking care of them (John 19:26-27).

When Proverbs 10:2 reveals, "Treasures gained by wickedness do not profit, but righteousness delivers from death," it teaches us that those who gain money unjustly are guilty of idolatry and are not walking with Jesus. After all, covetousness is idolatry (Col 3:5). Proverbs 10:4-5 warns about the disasters of laziness and the rewards of a good work ethic, which implies that laziness reveals a heart that does not follow Jesus (see also 1 Tim 5:8). Proverbs 10:12 demonstrates, "Hatred stirs up strife, but love covers all offenses." Properly applied, this verse helps us see that hatred is idolatry. Persons who cannot forgive a wrong against them are usually worshipping themselves. On the other hand, love forgives. Jesus by his love on the cross covered all offenses and demonstrated his willingness to forgive his enemies. If we are walking with Christ, then we should love in this way. Jesus is the Wisdom of God from Proverbs we are called to embrace. Proverbs is not a collection of tips for wise and easy living. Proverbs points the reader to a relationship with Jesus that enables us to walk in wisdom.

The Seventh Feature: Wisdom is the
Way the World Works

God created the world by wisdom (3:19-20; 8:22-30), so the cosmos is patterned after wisdom. There is a harmony to the world so that it works properly. Thus wisdom looks like perfect *shalom* between us and God, us and each other, and us with the world around us. There is an order to things so that they follow a certain pattern, a certain order. Wisdom is living in accordance with that order.

The problem is that the Fall messed up all of that harmony when man sought knowledge and wisdom apart from God. It plunged the whole world into the curse of death and the reign of Satan. Now, our vertical relationship with God is off, and so is the horizontal relationship with each other and the world around us. Our sin and foolishness has placed a barrier between us and God, but it has also placed a barrier between us and other people, and we have difficulty now perceiving the order by which the world works. Also, in the world's fallen condition, the patterns sometimes don't work immediately anymore. But, as we will see, Proverbs offers a way to change that.

Old Testament Background

Throughout the Bible, Wisdom is the means God uses to create. In the beginning, God used wisdom to build the world (Prov 3:19-20). In Exodus 31:1-2, he empowers the builders of the Tabernacle with wisdom. Indeed, the builders are given the Spirit *and* wisdom to build a dwelling place for God. Just as the Spirit hovered over the waters to create the world in Genesis 1, the Spirit is given to build a new cosmos in miniature—the Tabernacle that is patterned after creation. Later, he empowers Solomon with the Spirit and wisdom to build the Temple, which is also patterned after Eden (1 Kings 7*ff*). Isaiah prophesied that the Messiah would be anointed with the Spirit of wisdom and would bring a new order to the cosmos where things again work the way they did in the beginning (Isa 11).

Creation Order in Proverbs

In Proverbs, Wisdom builds the Creation (8:22-30) and her house—her Temple (9:1-6). Additionally, wisdom is to be used to build our homes (the loving families of 24:3). That is why wisdom is so valuable. The world works in a certain way. By pursuing wisdom, you can know that way and build your life in accordance with it so that you can succeed. In a fallen world, these precepts generally work out now, but they will always work out in the New Heavens and the New Earth. Wisdom gives one the ability to perceive the order and live by it. Having the Holy Spirit through regeneration helps one walk according to the pattern the Spirit built into the world.

God created the world in wisdom (a certain pattern), which causes the world to operate in a specific manner. Wisdom is living according to that pattern. Our sin and foolishness, however, keeps us from living in the proper manner. In order for sinners to again perceive that proper order, God must reveal the wise pattern of the world to us, which is exactly what he does in Proverbs. Fearing him is the grid through which we must view all of life. Christians must view the world through the lens of our covenant relationship with him and make observations about how the world works in light of that relationship.

Since there is an order to the Creation, living against that order is suicidal. It is life-denying to live against God's order. As a result, Solomon pleads with his son, and by extension, his readers, to observe the order and live by it. While our sin keeps us from perceiving this order, it is revealed in Proverbs and we are redeemed to perceive it. This order is why judgment is often pictured in Proverbs as reaping what has been sown. Those who reject Wisdom and the fear of Yahweh, will "eat the fruit of [their] way" (Prov 1:31). Yahweh built the world in such a way that certain consequences are inherent in certain actions. Wicked or foolish actions will lead to bad consequences and wise or righteous actions will lead to good consequences or rewards. Solomon tells his son to observe this reality in the world and live in light of it.

The examples of a Creation pattern in Proverbs are numerous since Solomon's wisdom empowered him to observe nature (1 Kings 4:33). This divinely empowered observation produced a number of illustrations that are employed in the Proverbs. Grabbing a stray dog by the ears is dumb because the dog will bite you, and so is getting into an argument that is not yours (Prov 26:17). Observing the work ethic of ants reveals that hard works leads to provision and laziness to poverty (Prov 6:6-11). The manner in which a dog licks up its own vomit is equated with repeating foolish decisions instead of learning from them (Prov 26:11).

To ignore this divinely inspired observation and explanation of how the world works is to invite destruction. God made everything. He knows how it works. He tells us how it works because he loves us and wants what's best for us (Prov 8:31). He is not trying to make our lives more difficult or less enjoyable with his counsel. He is trying to help us! We end up hurting ourselves when we choose to be autonomous from God; the same mistake our first parents made in the Garden. In essence, Proverbs is not just teaching us that sin is wrong, although it is, but also that sin is destructive and suicidal. Flee from sin. Submit to God's wisdom.

Not only does the world work in a certain way and not only do certain actions produce certain consequences, but God stands behind this order, upholding it, guaranteeing that it works out the way He has told us it will. "Will he not repay each person according to what he has done?" (Prov 24:12). Refusing the wisdom of Proverbs, or Scripture in general, will destroy your life. The destruction will be seen in negative consequences now. These consequences are merely a foretaste of the devastation that will come later at Final Judgment. Why? Judgment awaits all who reject Wisdom, because rejecting Wisdom is ultimately rejecting Jesus.

Fulfillment in the New Testament

Wisdom is personal, but so is the created order. The world was created by Jesus, and for Jesus, and Jesus upholds all of it with his Word (Heb 1:3). Indeed, Paul says that all things are being united in him (Eph 1:10). The pattern of the world is centered on Christ. That is, the world is meant to point us all *to* Christ. For example, the seasons point us to the gospel. During winter, all things die (i.e. plants, leaves, grass, etc.), but during spring they are raised from the dead to new life. The turning of the earth and the shifting of the seasons are meant to point humanity to Christ. Therefore, in order to perceive the order of the world presented in Proverbs, you have to know Christ because the order is personal. You can only view the world rightly through your relationship to him. Again, the vertical harmony with God through his Wise Son will lead to edenic harmony with your neighbor and the world around you.

How to Preach Christ

When preaching on the ant in Proverbs, or the dog who returns to his vomit, or someone who grabs a stray pit-bull by the ears, point out that the reason people are lazy, repeat their mistakes, and get into fights they have no business fighting is because they have a problem with Jesus. Jesus obeyed and fulfilled this wisdom by working to accomplish what the Father sent him to do, by growing in wisdom, and by knowing when to stay silent. It is only by growing in Christ that one will grow in wisdom, and part of wisdom is learning to view the way the world works through the lens of the gospel.[21]

The Eighth Feature: Wisdom is a Paradox Because It is Both a Gift and an Effort

Wisdom is a paradox because it is a gift given by God, but it is also a treasure that one must pursue. Finding wisdom is like going on a treasure hunt (2:4). Proverbs 2 also teaches that wisdom is a gift from the mouth of God (2:6). So, in order for someone to be wise, God must grant wisdom just as he granted it to Solomon (1 Kings 3). At the same time, one must also work hard to find wisdom.

The Paradox in Proverbs

How does this paradox unfold? It unfolds in two ways. First, the search for wisdom begins with the fear of Yahweh (1:7), *the* key component to wisdom in Proverbs. The one who would be wise must recognize that wisdom cannot be found within himself or herself. Instead, he or she must look to God in faith for it. Wisdom is a gift that God gives (Jas 1:5). Second, within the framework of a covenant relationship with God that enables one to view the world through the lens of his Word, one must observe the world, pay careful attention to the world, in order to be instructed in wisdom.

To grow in wisdom, a person must observe the way things work around us and understand these observations as parables that instruct us in the way the world works. We have seen this approach in the way watching ants and dogs instruct us about how to live. Another example is to survey how a fire dies when it lacks fuel. The conclusion drawn from this observation is that refusing to gossip will end a quarrel (Prov 26:20). Growing in wisdom takes grace-saturated effort to make sense of the world around us!

How to Preach Christ as the Fulfillment

The New Testament reveals a similar paradox with regard to our salvation. Salvation is all of grace, it is God's gift (Eph 2:8-9), but we are also to work out our salvation with fear and trembling (Phil 2:12). God demands our grace-saturated efforts in our walk with Christ. The power for the effort is his gift, but we must exert it nonetheless (Heb 13:21). We are called to make efforts and strive for peace and "for the holiness without which no one will see the Lord" (Heb 12:13), and if we don't then we haven't been saved. So wisdom, like the gospel of Jesus, is a gift that requires effort. When we preach the imperatives of Proverbs we should never rob them of their power as if we are not called to obey them. When we preach them, however, we should be careful not to mix up the order of events. It is God's gift of grace that enables the fool to pursue wisdom.

The Ninth Feature: Wisdom is Choosing the Right Path in Life

Proverbs repeatedly presents two paths in life and asks the son (and the reader) to choose one. The wise path leads to life and the foolish path leads to death (1:15;

2:8, 12-13, 20; 3:6, 17, 23; 4:11, 14, 19, 26; 5:8, etc.). Wisdom is concerned with the habit, the progressive conduct, of our lives. Are we progressing in maturity? Proverbs teaches that the path on which we walk reveals the person we are ultimately pursuing, either wisdom or folly.

The Path in Proverbs

Proverbs teaches that walking in wisdom in our daily lives is like walking a path. In this regard, Proverbs corrects many contemporary misunderstandings about "spirituality." Christians often try to compartmentalize spirituality by dividing the "spiritual" life from the "secular" life. Spirituality is pushed to the fringes and viewed as something intensely personal, even private. As a result, many see spirituality as what is done on Sundays, Wednesdays, or whenever they do "religious" things. The remainder of the week is viewed as sort of morally or spiritually neutral, concluding that God is not concerned with a lot of what happens throughout the week. That is, God really cares whether a person has a decent devotional time, but he is not as concerned about whether a person completes a work assignment as promised, turns in school assignments in a timely manner, or is a good listener in conversations.

We tend to think that God is concerned with whether or not we are a good witness at work (after all that's the really spiritual work), but we don't think God is so concerned with whether or not we fix the leaky faucet or pick up our room.

Proverbs obliterates such an unbiblical notion! Proverbs clearly reveals that God is concerned with the minute details of our daily lives. Proverbs shows that the details we often think are morally neutral are not so neutral after all. Wisdom is choosing between the two paths of life. One path is righteous and leads to life. The other path is wicked and leads to destruction. Properly understood, wisdom is a path or a course of life that we are progressively following or not. Wisdom is not a one-time gift or a mental level at which you arrive. The path you walk each day in the seemingly boring details of your life reveals whether or not you fear the Lord. At the end of the day, if someone has a temper, cannot control their tongue, or plan for the future, it is because that person does not fear the Lord. They are not wise.

Proverbs demonstrates that God is as concerned with the tidiness of your car or the completion of your assignments as he is with the quality of your devotional life. He says all of life is lived before him to bring him glory. In fact, the words "quiet time" and "devotional life" are never mentioned in the Bible. There is however a tremendous amount of instruction about laziness and many other seemingly mundane things that we often see as spiritually neutral.

The call to wisdom is the call to walk the path that avoids the pitfalls that lead to an early death and eternal judgment. Proverbs teaches when we travel this wise path we will not stumble (Prov 4:12). Instead, we will live a life of safety and security because the path of wisdom is smooth and avoids the foolish obstacles that ruin lives.[22] The struggle of fools is that they do not see the close connection between their foolishness and the disastrous consequences that come from it. The lazy person does not perceive how their habitual laziness has led them into poverty. The gossip does not see how their consistent gossip has cost them friends. The fool does not see how he is repeating the same mistakes constantly. Fools do not see that life is a path that leads somewhere. Our decisions are all connected, not isolated. Walking the right path is vital. It is the difference between life and death.

In Proverbs 4, Solomon urges the reader to embrace the *person* of Wisdom (4:5-9) and then walk the *path* of wisdom (4:11-19). Again, one must have a relationship with the person before he or she can walk the path. Proverbs teaches that the path of wisdom is progressive, like dawn increasingly growing stronger until there is full brightness. The moment a person begins to follow the proper path, wisdom can be seen only faintly. As we continue to follow this path, however, our vision improves. We are able to see better, clearer, and further. One day we will see completely clearly (4:18). Conversely, the fool walks in darkness, not seeing that his path leads to everlasting shame (4:19).

How to Preach Christ as the Fulfillment

Proverbs teaches that the path to wisdom is personal. The wise path is centered on Christ because Jesus is "the way" (John 14:6). You must believe in Jesus to walk in wisdom. The path you walk reveals the person you follow. Therefore, if you are following a path of foolishness, even in the seemingly neutral or mundane details of your life, then you are moving towards destruction, not just because there may be some unpleasant temporary consequences for your actions, but because your actions demonstrate that you are, in fact, moving away from Jesus Chris.

Consequently, when preaching Jesus from Proverbs we must teach our people that if they are not walking in wisdom in the practical areas of their lives (i.e. consistently speak without thinking), it is because they have a problem with Jesus and need to repent. If the details of our lives are not being conformed to the image of Christ as revealed in Proverbs, then we are not trusting properly in the promises of the gospel.

Wisdom, according to Proverbs, is a person to know and a path to follow. As one walks in foolishness he or she walks away from the Wisdom of God, who is Jesus of Nazareth. As Russell Moore has said, "You can have an amazing quiet time, but if you cannot control your tongue from saying too much, then you have an issue with Jesus. You can tear up at praise choruses, but if you nag your husband, then you have a problem with Jesus. You can be in three different Bible studies, but if you cannot clean your room when your parents tell you to, it's because you are walking away from Jesus."[23] God is concerned with every detail of our lives. He is committed to conforming us into the image of Wisdom, progressively and patiently. We all walk a path in life. The progressive character of our life reveals which path we are on. It reveals whether or not we are walking after or away from Jesus of Nazareth.

The Tenth Feature:
Proverbs are Promises

Scholars like to say that Proverbs are not promises; rather they are general truths that, all things being considered, usually work out.[24] But, that is not how Proverbs presents its wisdom. You can bank on this wisdom because these counsels are promises.[25] They are not always true immediately, but they are always true ultimately.

Promises in Proverbs

Proverbs makes lots of promises. Proverbs promises that the Lord will not let the righteous go hungry (10:3), that laziness leads to poverty (10:4), that a good work ethic leads to provision (10:4), and that being a person of integrity will keep you from disaster in your life (10:9). These statements often create interpretive dilemmas for the preacher. "What about the person who obeys Proverbs, yet does not receive the promised blessings?" There are many who do things the right way and still suffer. There are many who are wicked and still prosper. How are we to handle the exceptions to what Proverbs promises? The answer to this crisis of experience is not to ditch the notion that the Proverbs contain promises, but rather to recognize the fact that in a fallen world these promises are not always realized immediately. This reality is part of the crisis of wisdom that is seen in part in Proverbs and more fully in Ecclesiastes and Job. Sometimes people believe God, obey God, and still see life fall apart.

Obedient, wise Christians still get cancer, lose their jobs, or have kids walk away from the faith. Sometimes the plight of Christians is to suffer in the present and to receive our promised rewards only in the next life. God does not promise Christians their best life now; he promises our best life *later*. The sages who wrote Proverbs were not fools; they understand this reality. That is why the Proverbs are filled with so many "better than" sayings that show wickedness sometimes does prosper in this life. Proverbs also reminds the reader consistently that this reality will not always be the case. Waltke writes, "The several 'better than' proverbs assume that at present the wicked have material presents and the righteous do not: 'Better a little with righteousness than much gain with injustice" (cf. 16:8, 19; 17:1; 19:1, 22; 21:9, 19; 22:1; 25:24; 28:6; Ps. 37:16; Eccl. 4:6)."[26]

Proverbs are promises that are generally true now, but are always, ultimately, true later.[27] Even if those who pursue wisdom do not see the promises realized in this life, in the New Creation they will experience *every* spiritual and physical blessing.

Avoid approaching Proverbs as if it teaches a type of prosperity gospel. The problem with proponents of the prosperity gospel is that they assume godly people will never suffer in this life. That contention is not biblical. It certainly is not taught in the Proverbs! The Bible is clear that godliness is no guarantee that things will go well for us in this life. The Bible is equally clear that for those who follow Christ things will go well ultimately for you in the next life.

How to Preach Christ as the Fulfillment

The biggest problem with the prosperity gospel proponent's approach to Proverbs is that they bypass Jesus. The primary emphasis of their teaching is that if you obey you will be blessed and if you disobey you will miss out on blessing. But the question has to be asked, "Who is the obedient Son of Proverbs? Who walks in wisdom?" It certainly is not the reader. *Jesus* is the one who perfectly lived out the wisdom of Proverbs. Additionally he is the one took the judgment that fools deserve. He suffered in our place that we might be forgiven. Then, as the wise Lord of the universe, our redeemer, he shares the rewards of wisdom with those who believe in him.

If you are joined to Jesus Christ by faith, then God will credit Jesus's perfect covenant-keeping record to your account, and he will conform you into the image of his Son by the Spirit. As sons in Christ, we now live out the Proverbs by recognizing that life sometimes will work out now, but that it *certainly* will work out later. After all, Jesus walked in wisdom perfectly and died an early death. It appeared that following the way of wisdom did not really work for about three days—until he rose from the grave and walked away from the tomb. If wisdom does not seem to work out immediately, keep an eternal perspective! The Proverbs are promises, but they are given to Jesus because he is the one who keeps the wisdom of the book, and we can only receive them if we are united to him by faith.

The Bible reveals that Jesus is the Wisdom of God (1 Cor 1:24, 30). He is the fulfillment of the ideals of Proverbs (Isa 11:1-5) and of Woman Wisdom (Matt 11:19). He is the Greater Solomon (Matt 12:42). He is the son who grew in wisdom (Luke 2:52). Jesus is Wisdom in human flesh, the perfect embodiment of Proverbs. Jesus is the key to being wise. We can only be wise in daily life and for eternity by trusting in him and following him. We fall short of wisdom and deserve death, but Jesus was wise for us and took the punishment our foolishness deserves. Those who are united to him by faith receive his Spirit and will be conformed to his image. That is, you will be made like the "son" of Proverbs.

Chapter 4

Preaching Christ from Proverbs

I recently sat down with a young man who wanted to get some counsel. He had been dating the same girl for three years but was apprehensive about making the decision to marry her. He knew that it was the right decision eventually, but wanted to talk about timing, what God expected of him as a husband, and a host of other things. That kind of meeting happens all of the time. Almost on a weekly basis I will meet with someone who wants to ask me about God's will for their dating relationship, or for their job, or for what school they should attend, or a hundred other things. People want counsel for decision-making.

People are desperate to find practical advice for getting through their daily lives. That's why how-to books stock the shelves of your local bookstore, and Delilah After Dark always has full phone lines, and magazines on everything from how to have a better sex life to how to pick your fantasy football team fly off the racks. Christians are no different. We are desperate to know "God's will for our lives." We are desperate for strategies and tips on how to make everyday decisions from parenting our kids to managing our finances. The books, radio shows, and magazines that "Christian" industries produce are often just a baptized version of what the "secular" industries produce.

This reality is why Christians love the book of Proverbs. It seems so intensely practical. Much of it is easier to understand and to see its relevance for our daily lives than Leviticus, or Romans, or Hebrews. We love how-to strategies complete with boxes to check. But Proverbs is much more than that. Proverbs presents to its readers the path of wisdom that leads to life and the path of foolishness that leads to death. Thus, folly is more than immaturity or silliness; it is a failure to see the world clearly. Foolishness is walking a path that seems right to you at the time, but ultimately it leads to death (Prov 14:12). And wisdom is more than intelligence; it is an ability to see the way the world works. Wisdom is the skill to discern the difference between right and wrong, and that will lead to life!

Skill for daily living is important, but the first step to walking the wise path and avoiding the destructive consequences of foolishness is to recognize that wisdom is not first and foremost a collection of tips to learn and apply. Wisdom is a person that you need to trust. Proverbs presents two paths and two personas: Wisdom and Folly (Prov 9). They stand at the street corners and yell at you to listen to them—to embrace them. Whose voice will you listen to? The answer to that question will determine whether or not you are wise or a fool. And whether or not you adhere to the principles of wisdom laid out in Proverbs reveals which voice is influencing you. If you fail to meet the wisdom of Proverbs, it is because you are not listening to the voice of Wisdom who is Jesus of Nazareth. If you say things without thinking, if you give in to your child's temper tantrum for the latest toy, if you constantly spend money you do not have, and if you show up late to work and leave early, then it does not matter how many church programs you are involved in, you have a problem with Jesus. The Wisdom of God calls out to you with a Galilean accent, but do you hear him?

The answer to that question will determine whether you can live out the wisdom of Proverbs or not. The ten features of wisdom in Proverbs that this book has laid out come down to where you stand with Jesus. You do not have the wherewithal to rule your foolish appetites. You need Jesus the King-Sage to rule them. If you lack the ability to read people and situations, then the answer is not to simply try harder or grab a how-to manual off a bookstore shelf, but rather to embrace Jesus who produces this ability in his followers. If you lack the ability to determine the right ethical decision in your business, or with your marriage, then run to Jesus in repentance and faith. Trust and obey him because those are the essential components to the wise life. Whether or not you follow Jesus is a life and death matter because this is the way God created the world to work. Living against the wise pattern that God has woven into the fabric of the cosmos is suicidal. The world works a certain way, and you must perceive that in order to live according to it. Jesus is the one who created the world and who upholds it right now, so it is only through him that you can see how the world really works. Yes, we live in a fallen world where these patterns do not always work out immediately, but Jesus stands behind them to ensure that they will work out ultimately.

Since this is true, we must preach the wisdom of Proverbs to our congregations with Jesus as the central message. Our people will not be able to fight against their foolish appetites, or discern the motives of people, or decide between right and wrong in everyday situations, without first submitting themselves completely to Jesus Christ who is the wisdom of God. Whether or not our people live a life that avoids the pitfalls of stupid decisions ultimately comes down to what they have done with Jesus.

Yes, Proverbs deals with the practicalities of everyday life. It blows away the misconception that God is only concerned with your corporate worship life and your private devotional life. God has given us wisdom for everything—from the use of our words, to managing our finances, to parenting our children, to what kind of employee we will be. The good news for those of us who look at these directives and feel shame is that there is one who lived it out, and his name is Jesus. He freely offers to us not only forgiveness for where we missed the standard, but he also offers a new ability that we never had before—skill to live our everyday lives God's way. It is not enough to simply know what to do if we do not have the ability to do it, and that ability only comes through the gospel of Jesus Christ.

Appendix 1

Christ-Centered Sermon Examples from Proverbs

I am wholeheartedly committed to verse-by-verse expository preaching, and large sections of Proverbs are tailor-made for this type of preaching. Some sections of Proverbs, however, are much more difficult to preach in an expository manner due to the apparent random nature of their arrangement. It is proper, therefore to preach much of Proverbs thematically by grouping proverbs that deal with the same subject (i.e. money, parenting, marriage, use of the tongue, and work ethic). My approach to Proverbs is a hybrid of expository and thematic.[28] Even when I do thematic preaching, however, I want to preach expositionally and allow texts I choose to drive the sermon. By "thematic preaching," I do not mean an approach where one picks and chooses verses on a topic and strings them together to make a point. Rather, one should survey all of the verses in Proverbs on a given theme in order to let the book dictate its own teaching of that topic. This approach still allows the preacher to expound what Proverbs says while submitting to the theme of the book itself, not the preacher's arbitrary selection of verses.

Below is a collection of sermon notes from four sermons I preached from Proverbs. They are included so the reader can use them as a resource to help them think through how to preach Christ from the book of Proverbs. The first two examples are of expository sermons. The third example is of a thematic sermon on the topic of laziness in Proverbs. The fourth example shows how to preach on a single proverbial pair (Prov 26:4-5).[29] These are representative of the three types of sermons that can be preached from Proverbs.

Example 1: Proverbs 1:8-19

Introduction: In his book, *Counterfeit Gods*, Tim Keller tells the story of a French money-manager who invested the wealth of many of Europe's royal and leading families. He lost 1.4 billion of his client's money in

Bernard Madoff's Ponzi scheme. So in complete despair he slit his wrists in his Madison Ave office.[30]

- His greed to gain easy money through a get-rich-quick scheme destroyed his life!
- One truth illustrated quite clearly in our day is that "naked greed destroys!"
- The "Culture of Greed" is what brought about the economic collapse of 2008
- Greed has been destructive on our country, on companies (Enron), and individuals (destroyed families). We've wanted money at any cost, and we've PAID for it!

The problem for us is that we think this is only a problem for people on Madison Ave!

- We think this is a problem for really rich people – We can't see our own greed
- We think our pursuit of nice things is normal
- I've seen many families destroyed by the desire to accumulate nice things, but I've never had someone come to my office for counseling to confess, "My greed for money is destroying my family."
- They come to my office after the fact when it's too late
- We are too foolish to see our own greed – to see the trap we're setting for ourselves right now

- -his is as true for middle class America as it is for the "rich."

Transition: Solomon warns his son that greed will destroy him, and the Spirit warns us through Prov 1:8-19!

1. Getting Money the Wrong Way Will Destroy You

King Solomon (the father) instructs the crown prince (his son)

- He appeals, exhorts, pleads with his son to listen!
- Not only does the father want his son to listen to him, but he also says listen to the "law" of your mother (both parents are teaching)
- Parents are responsible to teach their children the "law" (good/evil) and wisdom (way life works)
- Don't abdicate this (dads!) or farm it out to teachers, coaches, agent Oso, etc.
- Teach your children how life works because you know what is best for them! (i.e. teach God's Word)
- Solomon doesn't just tell his son "what" to do; he also tells him "why" to do it (1:9)
- Good teaching never stops at the what; it always moves to the why
- It'll give you a "good life" – Jewelry is symbolic here of health, prosperity, and honor

Solomon turns to the specific life lesson he wants his son to learn > he gives a Parable/story (1:10-19)

- This story is similar to what happens to the Good Samaritan in Luke 10
- He tells his son of the temptation to join a gang (peer group), kill someone and take their money
- He pleads with his son: My son, don't be enticed by them! (don't be pressured by sinful peers!)
- He knows what that will lead to – it's common sense and something he has observed before!
- He warns his son not to walk in this "WAY" (1:15)
- Proverbs repeatedly presents 2 paths: 1) wise, righteous that leads to life AND 2) the foolish, wicked that leads to death
- Way has a double meaning here: 1) don't go with them (literal) and 2) don't follow this course of life (metaphor for the path that leads to death!)

He gives the outcome > Again, good teachers always give the WHY

- Their feet rush to shed blood (1:16) but it's not just the innocent's blood, it's also theirs (1:18)
- He uses the analogy of a bird and a net (1:17). The point is that even a dumb bird recognizes a trap if it's spread out in front of it. So, young man, if

a bird has enough sense to avoid an obvious trap, so should you!

- Robbers, you're dumber than birds because you're like a bird who sees a net and still flies into it!
- So, the father pleads with his son to recognize that this will end badly and wreck his life
- Their foolishness will turn back on them, so avoid it!

Then, Solomon gives the conclusion (1:19): so are the ways of everyone who is greedy for profit, it takes away your life!

- The principle is clear: getting money the wrong way (at other's expense) will destroy you!
- Using, abusing, manipulating, cheating, etc. to get money will end badly
- Greedy desire and craving for getting money quickly, easily and at any cost will DESTROY you!

2. Problem: It doesn't always work out immediately, but it will work out ultimately!

Most of us have a problem with this text, and it's a question, "Is this true?"

- We know stories of people who cheated and got away with it (unethical in business and got rich)
- We know those who used/abused others to get money and never got what was coming to them
- Perhaps we have gotten away with something (i.e. cheating on taxes)
- AND, we know stories of those who said "no" to bribes, refused to cheat, who did things the right way, kept their integrity and suffered for it! (didn't get rich, missed out, etc.)
- Illustration: I knew a missionary couple kicked out of Central Asia when they were denied the right business permit because they were the only business on the block who didn't bribe officials.

So, some people cheat and never face the consequences for it and other are honest and end up losing everything…so what now?! Is this Proverb true? Is it a promise?

- Yes! It generally works out NOW, sometimes it'll work out LATER, but it will eventually happen
- God created the world by wisdom so there is an order to things, and God stands behind his created order to make sure it happens…eventually!
- Illustration: Achan stole and was eventually found out, Ahab and Jezebel had Naboth killed, took his

vineyard, and didn't face the consequences until years later, but it did come!

The principle holds true: naked greed will destroy you...sometimes NOW, sometimes LATER!

- Your unethical business practice might be exposed and you go to jail or pay a massive fine
- You steal petty cash and get fired, you cheat on your taxes and get audited, etc.
- But, your greed may run your family into the ground and you might not see the toll on your wife and kids for years, but eventually you'll see it!
- It will happen, and if not uncovered in this life, it will be at Judgment!
- Any negative consequences that you receive immediately in this life are merely a foretaste of ultimate judgment

3. Problem: We've all failed!

We have a huge problem with this Proverb, and it's NOT whether or not it's true

- Our BIG problem is that we've all failed to live out the warning given by Solomon
- We've all walked in this foolish course of life and earned DEATH (wrecking our lives)

The problem is that we can so often read texts like this and comfort ourselves, "I've never been tempted to join a gang and kill someone to rob them…"

- That's true for most of us in this room…though probably not all of us
- The problem is that you think that fact absolves you of any guilt here, and you're wrong!
- You may never joined a gang, killed someone, and robbed them, but….

What about the principles this text is laying out?
- Have you ever given in to peer pressure to do something you shouldn't?
- Have you ever done something wrong to be accepted by the crowd?
- Have you ever been so lonely and desired community so badly you found it in wrong place?
- Have you ever used someone or manipulated someone to get what you want? To get money?
- Have you ever cheated the system to get money?

James the brother of Jesus tells us what leads to violence – he says it's unmet cravings!

James 4:1-2: What is the source of wars and fights among you? Don't they come from the cravings that are at war w/n you? You desire and do not have. You murder and covet and cannot obtain. You fight and war.

- Who among us has never craved this way?
- Some of you are running your family into the ground right now because of your craving to succeed in a job (Illustration: I had a friend in High School who looked so well-off in the eyes of the world. His dad owned multiple businesses. They lived in a huge house, and all of us loved to stay over there. But we'd see his mom passed out on the floor in front of the TV many nights driven into a drunken depression over a husband who never came home)
- Have you ever lied or cheated someone to make a sale?
- There may be some in this room who have had an abortion or paid for an abortion because of your craving to be "economically stable" or to live a life without stress.
- Who among us has never used someone to get something we want out of them?!
- Who among us hasn't stolen money from parents, government, employer (even if it's the time you waste on Facebook)?

We see this truth in children, don't we?

- Children will punch, kick, and scream to get the toy they want.
- Why? Because unmet cravings lead to violence
- As we grow, we don't bite anymore (usually) – we find socially acceptable ways to unleash our anger (backbiting, gossip, etc.), but the rage is still there when we don't get what we want.
- People boo and throw trash at refs who don't give their team the call, cuss and slam on the horn when someone pulls in front of you in traffic, fight over inheritance at funerals, etc.
- When we don't get what we want, we go into a rage (James says that's the root of murder)
- Have you been jealous of someone who got the promotion instead of you, so you badmouth them?
- The foolishness that Solomon warns against here is in all of us!

Wealth/gain (1:19) is a neutral term in Proverbs. It can be good or bad – depends on how you get it

- Proverbs is very positive about wealth if you get it by a good work ethic in order to provide for your family and be generous to the poor
- BUT, Proverbs is very negative about wealth gotten by the use of evil

- It condemns and warns about easy money/get rich quick schemes/using others to get what we want
- Proverbs 15:27: A greedy man brings trouble to his family, but he who hates bribes will live.
- This is true and we do it…whether it's taking a friend to lunch and saying "Ask me about my job and the company can pay for our lunch," or getting into pyramid schemes, or TV preachers who use "blessing" as a way to get people to send them money
- And, it's very easy for us to justify it: this is my money not the government's, my company doesn't "need" this money, I'm just trying to provide a little more for my family, etc.

Solomon warns his son to not have this course of life and the problem is we all fall into it

- We are all greedy for more…even if we consider ourselves poor, we still WANT more
- We don't care what it takes to get what we want or who gets hurt, we'll usually do it!

The scary part is that it will destroy you…you will reap what you have sown

- Might happen NOW: lose your job, lose your reputation, lose your family, etc.
- But, it will ultimately happen later at The Judgment because you followed folly instead of Jesus
- Eventually this will be exposed and will be your undoing! (i.e. bird going right for trap)
- 1 Tim 6:9 "People who want to get rich fall into temptation and a trap and into many foolish and harmful desires that plunge men into ruin and destruction."
- We've got a problem – we're heading for a trap, for death, and we can't even see it in ourselves like we see it so clearly in others
- No one sets out to wreck their lives and their families, but it happens.

4. Good News: Jesus can save you from your foolishness!

The entire Bible is about Jesus, including the Proverbs!

- Jesus is the SON who grows in wisdom and stature and favor with God and man (cf. Luke 2)
- Paul says that Jesus is the "Wisdom" of God for us (1 Cor 1:24, 30)
- Jesus is the one who can rescue us from our foolishness and make us wise

Amazingly, this Proverb/Parable plays out in Jesus' life

- Judas is enticed to join a gang who sets a trap for an "innocent" man (v.11)
- He does this to get money
- They set a trap and they take his life, and Judas gets a modest sum of money out of it

Jesus is executed (put to death) between two thieves (i.e. those who get money in the wrong way)

Again, it looks like this Proverb is NOT true:

- The innocent man dies the death that thieves deserve to die
- The guilty man lines his pockets

Judas threw in his lot with the gang to ambush an innocent man for profit, and it looked like he won, BUT by Sunday morning Judas is in the grave, and the Wisdom of God stands up and walks out of HIS!

- As John Mark McMillan says in his song "Death in His Grave": "On Friday a thief; on Sunday a king!"
- The gospel teaches that Jesus can rescue us from our foolishness
- Even though he was innocent he took the punishment greedy thieves deserve!

- Since he took the punishment we deserve, we can be forgiven of our greed if we believe!
- He gives his Spirit to his followers to empower them to walk in this wisdom
- He empowers you to avoid easy money, be content with what you have, and use your money to help others instead of using others to get money
- He gives us a new community who doesn't entice us to sin, but spurs us on to love and good deeds

Conclusion: The eschatological reward of wisdom is far greater than the ill-gotten riches that shimmer and fade and ultimately destroy. They're NOT worth it.

- Wisdom is the path to true riches
- And Wisdom isn't a thing at all; he's a person – Jesus of Nazareth!

Some do cheat to get money and never face the consequences in this life, and some are honest but lose everything…What now? Wait on the Lord, he will reverse the tables, sometimes he does it in 3 days, sometimes longer, but he will do it. What profit is it to gain the whole world and lose your soul?

Example 2: Proverbs 3:1-12

Introduction: I was an athlete who played 2 sports in High School, so I was in great shape

- BUT, I got out of shape after competitive sports ended because I didn't have that motivator anymore
- Solomon wants his son to be wise, but he knows he needs to MOTIVATE him towards wisdom

That's what he does in Proverbs 3:1-12. It's about being in a faithful covenant relationship with God

- Illustration: The covenant relationship of marriage where we make vows to one another
- The odd verses give the obligations for the HUMAN partner
- The even verses give the obligations for the DIVINE partner[31]
- READ Proverbs 3:1-12!

1. We Should Keep the Covenant (1, 3, 5, 7, 9)

The odd verse give the obligations that WE are called to live up to!

V. 1 "My Son" don't forget "MY LAW;" Let your HEART keep "MY" commandments

- The father (King Solomon) says to his son (the crown prince) "obey the law"
- Deut 4:6 says that obeying the law is Israel's "wisdom." Deut 6 says to teach the law to your kids. Deut 17 says the king is to be a man of the law in order to establish the kingdom. So, here Solomon is obeying Deuteronomy in teaching the law to his son in order to establish the kingdom. Wisdom is discerning right and wrong and obeying it in your daily life (daily living out the covenant)
- But, Solomon is clear that this isn't behavior modification. The law must be internalized in order to obey (let your heart keep them). There must be an inward transformation where the law is written on the heart (i.e. regeneration)

We see this in 3:3 as well – you can only obey the law by internalizing it (must be written on the heart)

- This is covenant language here (loyalty and truth)
- Bind them on your neck is Deut 6 language (i.e. bind the law on hand and frontlet b/t eyes)
- Write them on the tablet of your heart so you don't depart from it

- The 10 commandments were written on stone tablets, and the people didn't obey
- But, there's a promise that in the future the law will be written on the tablet of your hearts
- Then, you will obey
- Jer. 31:33 "But this is the covenant that I will make with the house of Israel after those days, says the LORD: I will put My law in their minds, and write it on their hearts;
- So, there's the need for inward-out transformation NOT behavior modification. God isn't after outward-in rule-keeping

This happens BY trusting the Lord instead of yourself (Prov 3:5, 7)…obedience to the law starts with faith

- This is the key to wisdom: Trust in Yahweh with all your heart and don't lean on your own understanding (i.e. trust God not yourself!)
- Proverbs says that foolishness is trusting your own heart and mind (28:26)
- Wisdom starts with recognizing that you don't have it and looking to God for it humbly

There is the wisdom of God and the wisdom of men, and they go against one another

- Proverbs says there's a way that seems right to man but in the end leads to death
- World says: it's wise to live together before marriage…how else will you know if you're compatible?
- God says: Doing a dress rehearsal for marriage with an out clause isn't the way to prep for marriage
- World says: it's wise to hoard your possessions
- God says: Prov. 11:24 One gives freely, yet grows all the richer; another w/holds what he should give, and only suffers want
- World says: It's wise to hold a grudge
- God says: do good to your enemy (Prov. 25:21-220
- World says: promote yourself
- God says: Prov. 27:2 Let another praise you, and not your own mouth…"

The key: don't be wise in your own eyes – that's the root of foolishness (cf. Gen 3)

- Instead, fear the Lord – revere him
- Foolishness = thinking you're wise (i.e. pride over humility)
- Submit to the Lord in all the areas of your life (i.e. morality, relationships, finances, parenting, job, etc.). Wisdom shows that the nitty-gritty details

of our lives are not "secular" and divided from the sacred. God is intimately concerned with them.

- Solomon gives the other side of the same coin of trust, which is repentance (3:7)
- Turn away from evil – recognize sin and foolishness in your life and turn from it to God!

Finally, Solomon gives 1 practical example of how inward piety leads to outward obedience to the Law

Generosity: honor the Lord with your possessions and your first fruits (3:9; cf. Lev 23:10; Dt. 18:1-5)

- Again, this is covenantal language – obey the law by giving back to the Lord out of what He's provided for you. Give the first fruits which means the best and first of what you have NOT the leftovers (app: give at the top of your budget not the bottom)
- This demonstrates gratitude for what God has given and confidence that he'll provide

2. God Blesses Covenant-Keepers (2, 4, 6, 8, 10)

We see the DIVINE partner's obligations in the even verses: He'll be a faithful rewarder

- 3:2 says "FOR" (i.e the Why/the motivation)
- Length of days, years of life, and shalom the law adds to you
- Obey dad and you'll live a longer life and a better life (similar to the 5th commandment)
- These are guidelines for healthy living that if you keep will prevent in most cases a wrecked life or an early death

Basically, Solomon is teaching that wisdom is the path to an abundant life and an eternal life

- Wisdom is a return to Eden where there is Shalom (things are the way they're supposed to be)
- There's complete harmony with God, other people, and the world around you!

3:4 says when covenant loyalty is written on your heart, then God will reward with his favor and a good rapport with others (i.e. right relationship with God and others)

3:6 says when you submit to God in all your ways, then he will make your paths straight. God will give you divine direction (i.e. his will as revealed in Scripture) to lead you on the right path in life.

3:8 says the reward is health – NOT being wise in your own eyes and fearing the Lord leads to health

- A well-ordered life leads to health (for example Prov. 5 warns of disease for sexual sin)
- These verses show that wisdom reverses the curse of sin, death and sickness (Eden!), whereas breaking the covenant leads to disease (Lev 26:16: visit you with wasting disease and fever)
- Faithfulness to the covenant leads to health as one of the blessings

3:10 says that when one honors the Lord with their wealth, then he will reward with full storehouses and vats that overflow with new wine (i.e. Provision)

- Again, this is covenantal language
- Deut 7:12-15 bless the fruit of your ground… take away from you all sickness
- If you obey, then things will go well: rain will come and the crops will grow, etc. (cf. Deut 11:14; 28:8; Mal 3:10), but the reverse will happen when you disobey (Deut 28:51)
- If you obey then God will give you more (enrich you)
- You may reap spiritual riches instead of physical ones, but often you receive both

- Illustration: When I was a freshman at the University of Kentucky, my parents were paying for my college tuition. If I had skipped class, not studied, and failed several classes, then my parents wouldn't have continued to support that. But, if I proved to be a good steward of what they were entrusting to me then I would continue to receive more. God works similarly. He entrusts good stewards with more.

3. This is Generally True Now, and Will Always Prove True Later (11-12)

Now, this raises an important question: Are these verses teaching a "prosperity gospel"?

- Trust God and obey him, and it'll lead to health, wealth, and happiness, right?
- YES! Just relax…I'm not going to turn into a TV preacher
- The problem is that this doesn't always work out immediately in a fallen world
- Sometimes you believe and obey, and it goes bad for you (get cancer, lose job, etc.)
- Sometimes we suffer NOW and receive the rewards only in the next life (Your best life later)

Proverbs are generally true NOW, but they are AL-WAYS ULTIMATELY true later

- In the New Creation, we'll experience every spiritual and physical blessing
- 3:11-12 help us understand that...you'll notice that I left them off earlier

Accept the Lord's discipline; don't despise or reject his correction (3:11)

- Don't get mad at the Lord when He allows discipline in your life
- Like your parents' discipline, the discipline of the Lord is for your good!
- We must have correction and discipline to be wise (that's the key to the book – humility)
- Left to ourselves we'll go down the wrong path!

The Lord's discipline may include disciplining sin, but not always because of sin (aka. Pruning)

- Discipline can be a positive thing; it's where we get the word for discipleship
- We workout – we discipline our bodies – we let hardship come in order to get in better shape
- We bring hard things on ourselves to prep us for much better

- Illustration: My daughter Maddy getting frustrated at homework, but now she can read!
- God allows hardship sometimes in our lives to produce something in us
- Deut 8: God gives us lean times so that we can be prepared to still trust in him in plenty!

WHY? Because he corrects those he loves like a parent. He does this for your good because he loves you

- If you don't discipline your child, then it's because you hate them
- Illustration: My dad had a friend in High School who told his buddies at dinner that he didn't have a curfew. All of the guys were jealous of him, but my dad said his expression changed right after he said it, he became somber, and said, "My dad doesn't care if I ever come home." He was crushed by the lack of discipline because it showed a lack of care.
- A loving parent won't let you go off on your own
- God corrects us because he loves us and wants what's best for us (ultimately to be made like Jesus)
- Author of Hebrews quotes this in chapter 12 – God allows suffering to produce holiness
- God is the rewarder – he doesn't always give you what you want, but does give what you need

- He'll do whatever it takes to conform you into the image of his covenant-keeping son so you can share in the blessings – the inheritance – of the sons of God
- So, sometimes you suffer now – you don't get the reward immediately – because he's molding you to prepare you for glory later!

The problem with TV prosperity gospel preachers is that they assume godly people will never suffer in this life, and that's unbiblical. Godliness is NO guarantee that things will go well for you in this life

- Just ask Job, and Jesus
- They will go well for you ultimately in the next life and be far better than the good life here
- Just ask Lazarus (Luke 16:19-31)

Transition: But the biggest problem with that approach to this text is that it bypasses Jesus. It doesn't ask the question, "Who has kept the covenant?"

4. The Gospel: Jesus kept the covenant for you

The prosperity gospel is a false gospel because it misunderstands that NONE of us are faithful covenant-keeping children. None of us have been perfectly obedient, trust God fully instead of ourselves, completely turned away from evil, been generous as we should, etc.

- This is talking about a covenant relationship b/t the Father and a son
- Israel is God's firstborn son but doesn't keep the covenant, neither does David, or Solomon, or his sons. Jesus is the SON who keeps the covenant!
- Luke 2:52 Jesus grew in wisdom and in stature and in favor with God and man (similar to Prov. 3:4!)

He represents us before the Father in this covenant relationship (He lives up to the obligations for us)

- He takes the curses/judgment for covenant-breakers (early death, sickness, sorrows, etc.)
- He offers us full forgiveness, credited righteousness, and the blessings for covenant-keepers alone!
- If you are united to him by faith, then God will conform you into his image
- As Romans 8 tells us…sometimes through discipline (famine, peril, sword, etc.)!

As the sons of God through Christ, this is NOW how we are to live and how we can live

- But, we recognize all the time that if it doesn't work out now…it will work out later
- In Christ, then law is on our hearts so we can obey, trust the Lord, live generous lives, etc.
- This is how God's sons live!

Conclusion: The problem with the prosperity gospel is NOT that it wants you to be physically blessed because God does too. The problem is that it misunderstands a fallen world, it bypasses Jesus, and it doesn't give us enough prosperity. It gives a prosperity that only last decades at the most.

Jesus is faithful to the covenant, but his life was cut short in the short run so his "days could be prolonged" later (Isa. 53:10; cf. Prov. 3:2). That's a BETTER reward…one where you never die again.

Come to him, be made like him, and be prepared to share in the blessings with HIM!

Example 3: Laziness

Introduction: Kenny Chesney sings a song called "Down the Road." It's about a boy who wants to marry a girl.

One of the lines in the chorus goes: "Her momma wants to know am I washed in the blood or just in the water; her daddy wants to know if I make enough to take his daughter down the road"

- We hear that and think those are 2 very different concerns
- Momma's is a very spiritual (and godly) concern whereas daddy's is a material concern
- WRONG! Wanting to know if a man has a good enough work ethic to provide for your daughter is a very spiritual concern according to the Bible
- Work is NOT a secular or neutral matter...it has everything to do with your walk with Christ.

Proverbs says that sloth – laziness – isn't just a character flaw; it's a SPIRITUAL problem!

- Proverbs MOCKS lazy people repeatedly...says they can't even bring food to their mouths
- Proverbs WARNS the lazy and calls them to repentance...READ Proverbs 24:30-34

1. Our Laziness is Destructive

This passage has a wise man that sees the field of a sluggard.

- Literally the text says that the man "lacks heart" (24:30 translated by ESV as lacking "sense")
- To lack a heart in the Bible is a SERIOUS spiritual problem
- His laziness shows because the field is overgrown with thorns
- Compare this with the curse language in Gen 3… sin makes it difficult to work and provide!
- Our sinful reaction to the curse is often to take on as little responsibility as we can (be a couch potato, have no drive, etc.)
- The sluggard gives into this…he's not sweating and he's not providing. He just lets the thorns grow and allows things to fall apart

The sage observes this and is instructed by it (25:32).

- There's an ORDER to the world so that it works in a certain way
- We see this in Prov. 6 when the sage observes the ants' work ethic to provide and store up
- You can see this behavior and observe its destructively negative consequences
- The sage is pleading with us to not live against the grain
- You can become the slob on the couch who is dependent on handouts (self-inflicted poverty)

- If you don't do what needs to be done, if you sleep too much, then your life will be in chaos and more likely than not you will be poor and unable to provide
- We need to be instructed by this as well and be called to a strong work ethic that enables us to meet our family's needs

BUT, the problem for us is that when we read these verses we automatically think of the 35 year old sleeping on his mom and daddy's couch watching Jerry Springer while he stuffs his face with chips!

- Some of you may be struggling like that, but not most of us!
- But, that image enables you to say, "I don't struggle with laziness!"
- Yet, we all have this tendency in our hearts and we don't recognize it because we measure ourselves against people that we KNOW are lazy.

- Some of you may be struggling with wanting your needs met without having to work for it or spend wisely. You depend on handouts.
- We have a slothful, yet entitled society that wants others to work for what they get.
- We see this in church all of the time with people who drive from church to church in town to see

if they can get money and know how to work the system.

- Prov. 20:4 - A sluggard does not plow in season; so at harvest time he looks but finds nothing.
- Problem: that's not most of us, so we don't think we struggle with this, BUT...

- Some people have a problem not prioritizing what NEEDS to be done over what we want to be done!
- This type of slothfulness is choosing to do what you want to do over what you need to do.
- Your life is a mess because you're not taking control (cluttered work space, fast food wrappers all over your car, etc.)

- Some people just love to sleep too much.
- That's a temptation for all of us because the God-ordained rhythm of work and rest can be abused.
- So, get out of bed and get to work.

Transition: but for many, it's not a LACK of activity; it's just the wrong kind of activity!

- Some people don't complete the tasks that are assigned to them or don't finish them on time.

- You're the kind of person who gets real excited about new projects, but you don't complete them or you're having to constantly ask for extensions.
- Proverbs 12:27 The lazy man does not roast his game.
- This hilariously pathetic image is of a man who hunted down some game but won't do the work to finish what he started and make the meal.

- Most people struggle with laziness by being side-tracked by all kinds of diversions.
- Like the guy in the movie "Office Space" who says, "In an average week, I'd say I only do about 20 minutes of real actual work."
- Why? Because you're checking Facebook all day, passing around YouTube clips, call in sick when Call of Duty is released, etc.
- I saw a stat a few years ago that said 400,000 workdays are lost EVERYDAY because people are playing angry birds!
- I retweeted that and a Facebook friend commented on my post by saying, "At least 15 people I work with are playing Angry Birds continuously while they talk to customer 7 hours a day."
- **Proverbs 12:11** He who tills his land will have plenty of bread, but he who pursues vain things lacks sense.

- Some people just constantly procrastinate on work.
- They start assignments the day before they're due.
- They put things off.

- Some people are all talk and little action.
- You meet and make big plans but you don't follow through.
- It's the husband who constantly says to his wife "I'll fix that" but never gets around to it.
- **Proverbs 14:23** All hard work brings a profit, but mere talk leads only to poverty.
- Don't say you'll do something if you won't.

- Some people don't take the initiative to provide for their family.
- Maybe it's child support, or claiming some illegitimate disability, etc.
- It's UNGODLY.
- The Bible isn't condemning those who are laid off or have a true disability.

- Some folks just make excuses to avoid work or to delay having to do it!
- **Prov. 26:13** The sluggard says, "There is a lion in the road, a fierce lion roaming the streets!"
- This guy makes a weak excuse to avoid work (but it seems viable to him).

- Illustration: I used to get up at 4AM to run with my youth pastor, but I would LOVE the mornings it rained because it gave me an excuse not to run. It was the best of all worlds because I didn't feel guilty about bailing because "I can't do it anyways." (I could've gone to the gym instead!)
- It's the same with excuses for work. People who ask for benevolence help tell me all the time, "I'll do any job that's available. I just want to work." Then I say, "Ok. I know the manager at the grocery store over on Main. I can get you a job tomorrow stocking shelves." Then, they'll say, "Oh, I can't do that because I have a back problem." They say they'll do anything, but then they shoot down EVERY job idea I give them. It's an excuse to not work!
- The best scenario (in our own minds) is to be able to convince ourselves that we are hard workers without having to actually expend the energy to be 1!
- **Prov. 26:16** The sluggard is wiser in his own eyes than seven men who answer discreetly.
- That's one of the keys about being lazy – you often don't know that you are!

This is a destructive path – NOT just because it'll embarrass you, although it will.

- NOT just because it'll make it difficult for you to give your family what they need, though it will.
- NOT just because it'll make you a drain on the people around you, though it will (cf. Prov. 10:26).
- BUT, it's destructive because ultimately it'll send you to Hell (the wages of laziness = Death!)
- The desire for ease, comfort, and to avoid work KILLS you.
- Proverbs 21:25 The desire of the lazy man kills him, For his hands refuse to labor.
- Again, it may not work out immediately because some lazy people inherit wealth, but it will work out ultimately.

Prov. 15:19 The way of the sluggard is blocked with thorns, but the path of the upright is a highway.

- Again, it's NOT just that you'll have difficulty making your way in this life as a lazy person, although you will, but there are 2 PATHS/WAYS that lead to 2 different DESTINATIONS.
- 1 leads to life and the other to death (and laziness is the path to Hell).
- Prov. 18:9 He who is slothful in his work is a brother to him who is a great destroyer (i.e. Satan).

- Judgment will fall. Sloth is not just ridiculous; it's destructive!

2. Our Laziness Points Us to Jesus

Laziness can be a sign of not being born again – lacking the new heart – and needing to be transformed

- This is why Paul says to deal with this in the church (if you don't work, then you don't eat)
- 1 Timothy 5:8 But if anyone does not provide for his own, and especially for those of his household, he has denied the faith and is worse than an unbeliever.
- If you don't have a work ethic, then there's no evidence that your faith is real (you're not believing the gospel).
- You may get up early, sit in your favorite chair and read Scripture for an hour, but if you constantly procrastinate on your work assignments or can't complete tasks that are assigned to you, then you have a problem with Jesus…it doesn't matter how long your quiet time is!

Solomon is pointing us to Jesus – the Wisdom of God (1 Cor. 1:30)

- This pattern observed by the Sage is centered on Christ who upholds the world right now.
- Laziness or work ethic shows if you're walking toward or away from Jesus.
- One way to know if you're walking with Jesus or not is to look at your work ethic (1 Tim 5:8).
- The Wisdom of God on earth had a job as a carpenter…he learned and worked a trade.
- He also did the work his Father sent him to do (John 4:34 "I must finish the work of Him who sent me." John 17:4 "I have finished the work which You have given me to do")
- God worked to create the world and provide for humanity. He worked 6 days and finished his task, and then he rested. Jesus also worked 6 days on Holy Week, said "It is finished" on day 6 when he completed the work of New Creation, and then he rested in the Garden Tomb on the 7th. He did this to provide for us what we can't provide for ourselves.

The response to laziness in our lives is to turn away from it to Jesus who perfectly imaged the Father by working. He died for all of us who fall short in work ethic and offers us forgiveness and escape from Hell.

- Then, he transforms us by his Spirit into his Image…the image of one who LABORS!

- God worked to create, produce, and provide food and a home for his children (cf. Gen 1-2).
- Part of being made in his image means that we do the same.
- We've failed, and the image is now distorted, but it's still there.
- Wisdom in Proverbs works and builds creation (Prov. 8) and a house (Prov. 9).
- Jesus worked to create, he upholds the Universe right now, and he worked to make all things new. He prepares a home for his family (John 14), and he feeds them (John 6).
- Being saved means being conformed into the image of Christ, and that means work/production.

Application: This means work in terms of vocation but also non-vocation

We are called to produce NOT just consume

- Proverbs talks about women who order the chaos and build homes (Prov. 14:1; Prov. 31).
- So, decorating, cleaning, consigning, changing diapers, and much more are not menial tasks, but rather are the way of wisdom (the way of Christ).
- This means that in the Body of Christ, we are called to serve.

- This means that Christians should be the BEST employees…Managers and bosses around town should call me and ask for more of our people!

This is important for all kinds of reasons, and one is what God is preparing you for in this!

Proverbs 12:24 The hand of the diligent will **rule**, But the lazy *man* will be put to forced labor.

- This doesn't just mean that you'll be promoted, although it does…
- Humanity was called to RULE the Creation in the beginning, but we handed it over to the Serpent. Solomon tells his Son – a Son who will rule Israel –good work ethic is necessary to rule.
- This is fulfilled in the Greater Solomon who not only rules Israel but the whole world.
- He regains what is lost in Eden and one day his kingdom will cover the entire COSMOS.
- Jesus says: those who are faithful in the small things will be put in charge of many things (Matt 25). And, he says his followers will rule the universe with him, but in order to do that we are called to be faithful in the seemingly mundane things.
- As Russell Moore says, "We are in an internship for the eschaton right now"[32].

- As you change diapers, set up chairs, carry out the project assigned by your boss, deliver the package, paint the wall, you are being prepared to be a king and queen of the universe.

Conclusion: We were called in the beginning to have dominion over the creeping things. Now, in our fallen condition – in our lack of dominion over our lives – God says look to the smallest of creeping things to learn it. Look to the ant you sluggard. This is an indictment that proves we NEED Jesus. We need to be made like him through the gospel.

Example 4: Proverbs 26:4-5

Introduction: Life is full of contradictions, and many of them are hilarious!

- Dolly Parton said, "It costs a fortune to look this cheap"
- Yogi Berra said, "No wonder no one comes to this restaurant anymore, you can't ever get a table"
- My daughter wants to be fiercely independent (cook for herself, take out the trash, etc.), but she wants me to carry her up the stairs when it's bedtime.

We are fallen creatures, so we all have our own contradictions and inconsistencies

- BUT, it's one thing for US to have contradictions; it's another thing to charge God with them!
- You can google "contradictions in the Bible" and find tons of lists
- It's a popular charge against Christianity
- People want to show the Bible is inconsistent, so they can prove that it is NOT God's Word, and therefore they don't have to take its claims seriously (i.e. John 14:6)
- These so-called contradictions are an attempt to turn people away from the faith
- Most of them are EASILY addressed to be honest
- BUT, we want to look at a common 1 here in Proverbs 26:4-5
- Even in ancient times, the Talmud notes an AP-PARENT contradiction
- **Read the Text**

Is the Bible contradictory, and therefore untrue? NO! So, what does it mean? Doesn't it seem to contradict? This is only an APPARENT contradiction NOT a real one.

- Some try to solve the dilemma by saying Proverbs aren't timeless or absolutes

- They are general rules that are RELEVANT to a given situation
- BUT, that's wrong…Proverbs are ABSOLUTE truths!

The sages who collected Solomon's proverbs were NOT stupid – they were WISE men

- Why would they put these 2 verses right next to each other?
- Because they're showing that they must be read TOGETHER
- Together – not separately – they give the true picture of reality (i.e. how to correct a fool)

1. Don't Stoop to the Fool's Level by Playing His Game

There are some types of fools and situations where you shouldn't rebuke, correct, confront, or answer

- Wisdom is the discernment to read the person/situation and know if that's the case
- How do you know? If your answer to them will require stooping to their level, then avoid it
- If your answer or attempt at correction will do no good, if it will drain your energy and not get anyone anywhere, then it's best to remain quiet.

- Prov. 9 says something similar. If despite your best efforts, they won't be corrected, if you only hurt yourself by playing his game, then stay quiet
- There are people who will ask you questions but don't really want to hear your answers because they think they know it all. Don't waste your time thinking through and answering their questions, emails, Facebook posts, etc.

I think 26:4 also means to NOT answer a fool in a foolish way…don't lie, exaggerate, mock, or speak unkindly just to get your point across.

- Example: You have to win the argument and shut them up, so you exaggerate to make the point
- Don't fight fire with fire…otherwise you are on the level with the fool
- AND, no honor is given to the fool (26:1)33 and he is under judgment.

So, there are some people you shouldn't answer/correct/keep the conversation going

Don't play his game or by his rules > if you're going to answer, then change up the rules!

- APP: For example in evangelism, you need to recognize sidetracking comments, don't play the game, keep the focus on Jesus' not objections about manuscripts…
- But, this is true in any type of conversation, dialogue or relational interaction
- Family, Church, Office, Neighbor, Classmate, Facebook, Blogs, Friends, Education, etc.
- Any counseling (pro or just advice) > wherever conversing takes place

APP: Refuse to play the fool's game with him!

- So easy for us to get sucked into responding on Facebook because want to be seen as right (let it go)
- Like the guy who tried to convince me one time that Jesus would've dated non-Christians
- That's NOT even worth responding to. Don't let someone get a rise out of you. Don't get into never ending arguments where you have to have the last word (in marriage, or a friendship, etc.)

Transition: BUT, don't use this as an excuse to chicken out because there is a time to answer…

2. Correct a Fool So He Doesn't Think He is Wise

26:5 says that there are some fools and situations that should be confronted, answered, or corrected.

- Don't stay quiet in those cases
- Because if you don't answer them, they'll be wise in their own eyes and destroy themselves (26:12)
- For some, it will do good to correct them because they might listen!
- Also, there are times when there are others around who'll be hurt by the person's foolishness, so you can't stay silent
- Don't tolerate foolishness in such a way that the person thinks what they're saying is right
- So, lovingly correct them – show their folly – without lowering yourself if it will do the person or others good.
- Otherwise, they might think they're smart because no one is correcting them
- This is true in BIG matters like evangelism, marital issues, etc., but it's also true in "little" matters like spending, laziness, bad thinking on a specific subject, etc.
- You will regret not speaking up when you had the chance if they hurt themselves

3. Wisdom is the Discernment to Know When to Correct

The sages' point is this: Wisdom is the discernment to read people and situations and know when to respond and when to stay silent

- Wisdom = growing in the knowledge of when to correct someone and when not to
- You're discerning the outcome – you know when answering will help him or play his game
- Daily life has both situations, and wisdom is the ability to assess them and decide what to do

Proverbs has taught us that Wisdom isn't a thing; Wisdom is a person – Jesus of Nazareth

- So, growth in him doesn't just mean growth in not sinning as much, although it does...
- It also means growth in DISCERNMENT!
- You know if answering will get you nowhere, or if it'll help the person or others around them!
- This is what growing in Christlikeness looks like

4. THE Power to Grow in Discernment is in Christ Not in You

NOT having this discernment reveals a problem with Jesus in your life

- You're not walking with him – you have an idol in your life
- If you're too cowardly to confront, or if you're not able to read a situation and know when to let it lie, then it's because you're not believing in Jesus rightly!

After all, Jesus AMAZED people with this ability. He knew when to stay silent because a reply would do no good. And, he knew when to correct. He could read people and situations and knew exactly how to respond or not respond

- In Matt 15, the Pharisees challenged him because his disciples didn't follow the rules
- He turns around and busts them for not honoring their moms and dads – He revealed their hypocrisy, so that they were not wise in their own eyes or the eyes of the crowd
- In Matt 16, Peter foolishly rebukes Jesus concerning the cross, and Jesus answers him to correct his folly, "Get behind me Satan!"

Look at Matthew 22:15-22…Jesus is able to know when they're testing him, and the opponents marvel at him, so that the text says in 22:46, "And no one was able to answer Him a word, nor from that day did anyone dare to ask him any more questions." (WOW)

- Jesus knew when to stay silent and refuse to play their games (Matt 21:27)
- When he's on trial with the Jewish leaders, he remains silent…he later amazes Pilate by this (Mark 15:5)

Conclusion: Jesus grew in this ability and this is what he produces in his followers

- They couldn't resist Stephen's wisdom (Acts 7:10)
- So, if you're NOT growing in this ability, then repent and go to Jesus
- Cry out to him, "Lord, show me where I lack discernment. Judge me in this and give me wisdom" (i.e. James 1)
- It could be because you're not a believer and need to trust him for the first time
- It might be because you are a believer but not walking with Christ in this area
- The answer is the same for both…repent and believe!

Appendix 2

Helpful Resources for Preaching Christ in Proverbs

I often get asked about the best resources for preaching and teaching Proverbs. There are many helpful ones out there, so here I try to list some that have been most helpful to me.

Commentaries:

- Bruce Waltke's 2 volume in NICOT – This is the best and most comprehensive work on Proverbs out there. It is a very scholarly but accessible and pastoral work. If one wanted to attempt a completely expository approach to Proverbs, then Bruce Waltke is extremely helpful. His commentary argues for textual unity instead of randomness, and he provides a way to do this.

- Tremper Longman's 1 volume in the Baker Commentary on the Old Testament and Psalms – This is the best commentary for preaching Proverbs because it combines scholarly, theological and pastoral insights in a relatively concise 1 volume. Also, it has a topical appendix at the back that breaks down some of the main subjects in Proverbs. This appendix provides a summary of that particular subject in the book as well as a list of verses that touch on it. This is very helpful for thematic preaching of Proverbs.

- Graeme Goldsworthy's *The Tree of Life* – This commentary is difficult to get your hands on, and if you want a thorough treatment of every verse in Proverbs, then this is not the commentary for you. But, if you are looking for a commentary that gives you tools for a Christ-centered approach to Proverbs, then this is the best commentary for you.

- Duane Garrett in NAC – This is very helpful and succinct.

- Roland Murphy in NIBC – This one is shorter, cheaper and more accessible then his Word Biblical Commentary.

- Derek Kidner in Tyndale – This is also succinct and helpful.

- Steinmann in Concordia – This work is large and expensive, but it also attempts to address Proverbs in a Christ-centered manner.

Audio:

- Russell Moore "Walking the Line" - This is the best overview and Christocentric presentation of Proverbs out there. http://www.russellmoore.com/resources/proverbs/
- Bruce Waltke "Fundamentals for Preaching Proverbs" at DTS- This is a very helpful intro to preaching Proverbs. Again, if one wanted to preach strictly expository messages through Proverbs then this is the place to start! http://www.dts.edu/media/people/?namekey=Bruce%20_Waltke

Other:

- Tremper Longman, *How to Read Proverbs* – Great overview of how to approach the book as well as how it points to Christ.
- Peter Leithart, *Wise Words* – The message of Proverbs presented as children's fairy-tale like stories. A GREAT resource for parents.
- Graeme Goldsworthy, Gospel and Wisdom – a gospel-centered approach to Proverbs.
- Jimmy Scroggins, "3 Circles" - While this video does not address Proverbs specifically, it does pro-

vide a good framework for approaching sermons in the book. God has a design for everything in the world, what Proverbs would call "wisdom," and we have all sinned against that design and are therefore broken. But, forgiveness and an ability to pursue God's design is available in the gospel of Jesus Christ. Therefore, when preaching in Proverbs on the use of the tongue, or finances, or a dozen other things, one could approach it using this gospel-grid. http://www.namb.net/video/3circlesguide/

Appendix 3

An Approach to a Sermon Series on Proverbs[34]

Expository Sermons[35]

- Sermon 1- Proverbs 1:1-7 "The Introduction"
- Sermon 2- Proverbs 1:8-19 "Avoid Greed At All Cost"
- Sermon 3- Proverbs 1:20-33 "Wisdom is a Person Not a Thing"
- Sermon 4- Proverbs 2:1-22 "Whose Voice Will You Listen To?"

- Sermon 5- Proverbs 3:1-12 "Does Proverbs Promise Too Much of the Wrong Thing?
- Sermon 6- Proverbs 3:13-35 "Blessing and Cursing"
- Sermon 7- Proverbs 4:1-19 "Wisdom is a Person and a Path"
- Sermon 8- Proverbs 4:20-27 "Your Heart is the Command Center for your Life"
- Sermon 9- Proverbs 5-7 "Honey Lips"
- Sermon 10- Proverbs 8:1-36 "Wisdom is Jesus"
- Sermon 11- Proverbs 9:1-18 "Which Invitation Will You Accept?"
- Sermon 12- Proverbs 10:1-11:31 "The Righteous, The Wicked, and Their Fate"[36]

In addition to preaching the sections that lend themselves easily to verse-by-verse exposition, one can preach thematic or topical series in Proverbs. In this approach you can group the proverbs on a particular theme or topic. These are shorter series that can be preached during specific times of the year or to help with special emphases. I enjoy preaching these kinds of series between series on biblical books. Here are some of the potential series:

Keys to Interpreting Proverbs:

- Sermon 1- "The Importance of the Heart for Wisdom" (Prov 4:23)

- Sermon 2- "Fear of the Lord vs. Fear of Man"(Prov 29:25)
- Sermon 3- "Humility vs. Pride" (Prov 11:2)
- Sermon 4- "Learn From Your Mistakes" (Prov 26:11)
- Sermon 5- "The Word of God" (Prov 30:1-6)

Riddle Me This: Unlocking the Hard Proverbs

- Sermon 1- Proverbs 22:6 "Train Up a Child…"
- Sermon 2- Proverbs 26:4-5 "Answer a fool; Don't answer a fool"
- Sermon 3- Proverbs 12:21 "The Righteous Don't Suffer or Go Hungry?"
- Sermon 4- Proverbs 30:11-33 "The Numerical Sayings"

Words: The Power of the Tongue

- Sermon 1- "The Heart is the Command Center of the Tongue" (Prov 4:20-27)
- Sermon 2- "The Power of the Tongue" (Prov 18:21 and others)
- Sermon 3- "Harmful Speech" (i.e. lying, gossip, slander, and more)
- Sermon 4- "Shut Up: Listening is Better Than Speaking"
- Sermon 5- "How to Confront Wisely"
- Sermon 6- "Prayer"

Relationships

- Sermon 1- "Wise Manhood" (i.e. Men as husbands, dads and workers)
- Sermon 2- "Wise Womanhood" (i.e. wives, moms and homebuilders)
- Sermon 3- "The Results of Wise Parenting: A Happy Home is Better Than a Wealthy Home"
- Sermon 4- "Instructing and Correcting Children"
- Sermon 5- "Friends: The Company You Keep" (Prov 13:20)
- Sermon 6- "Social Justice: How Do You Treat the Poor and Vulnerable?"

Money

- Sermon 1- "In God We Trust Not Money" (Prov 11:28)
- Sermon 2- "Generosity vs Stinginess"
- Sermon 3- "The Wise Use of Money: How to Spend, Save, and Invest for the Future"
- Sermon 4- "Your Fate is More Important Than Your Fortune"

The 7 Deadly Follies

- Sermon 1- "Wrath"
- Sermon 2- "Greed"
- Sermon 3- "Sloth"
- Sermon 4- "Pride"

- Sermon 5- "Lust"
- Sermon 6- "Envy"
- Sermon 7- "Gluttony"

Notes

1   Unless otherwise indicated, all Scripture quotations are from the The Holy Bible, English Standard Version® (ESV®), copyright ©2001 by Crossway, a publishing ministry of Good News Publishers. Used by permission. All rights reserved.

2   See Daniel Block's post on Christ-centered preaching where he says, "Few proverbs in the book of Proverbs speak of Jesus." http://www.christianitytoday.com/edstetzer/2013/june/christ-centered-hermeneutics.html?paging=off. Accessed February 14, 20014.

3   There are basically 7 collections of proverbs in the book. Bruce Waltke, The Book of Proverbs 1-15, NICOT (Grand Rapids: Eerdmans, 2005), 10.

4   Tremper Longman's work on Proverbs heavily influenced this portion of the chapter. Longman makes the case that Wisdom personified in Proverbs stands for Yahweh. The New Testament ultimately reveals that Wisdom is Jesus. Longman also argues convincingly that Folly personified in Proverbs represents idols or Satan ultimately. See Tremper Longman III, Proverbs, Baker Commentary on the Old Testament Wisdom and Psalms (Grand Rapids: Baker, 2006), 215-223.

5   In Sodom, Lot tells the two angels not to spend the night in the square and takes them to his house. Then, the men of the city tell Lot concerning his guests, "Bring them out to us, that we may know them" (Gen 19:5). At Gibeah, an old man tells the traveler and his concubine not to spend the night in the square and takes them to his house. The men of the city tell the old man concerning his guests, "Bring out the man who

came into your house, that we may know him" (Judges 19:22).

6   Proverbs points humanity to what was lost in the Garden of Eden. The wisdom of Proverbs offers the knowledge of good and evil, the tree of life, and human dominion.

7   God also granted wisdom to the builders of the Tabernacle, which was a precursor to the temple (Exod 31:1).

8   Solomon warns his son repeatedly in Proverbs to avoid the "foreign" woman (2:16; 5:10, 20; 6:24; 7:5).

9   The future establishment of the Davidic Kingdom in Proverbs is the thesis of my dissertation. For a detailed argument of how Proverbs functions in this way, see Jonathan Akin, "A Theology of Future Hope in the Book of Proverbs" (PhD diss., The Southern Baptist Theological Seminary, 2012).

10   I have been greatly helped in this section by Gary Tuttle. See Gary Tuttle, "The Sermon on the Mount: Its Wisdom Affinities and Their Relation to Its Structure," Jets 20, no. 3 (1997): 213-230.

11   Francis Brown, The Brown-Driver-Briggs Hebrew and English Lexicon, fifth printing (Peabody: Hendrickson, 2000), 416.

12   I give my full sermon outline on this text in Chapter 4 below.

13   James Hamilton, God's Glory in Salvation through Judgment: A Biblical Theology (Wheaton: Crossway, 2010), 834-836, ibooks.

14   For example, Eve eats the fruit because she thinks it is "desirable to make one wise" (Gen 3:6). Also, the tree of

the knowledge of good and evil is in the middle of the garden. Previously, I have argued that it is knowledge that Proverbs grants the reader. Finally, the tree of life is there as well. The tree of life is only mentioned in three books of the Bible: Genesis, Proverbs, and Revelation (Gen 2:9; 3:22, 24; Prov 3:18; 11:30; 13:12; 15:4; Rev 2:7; 22:2, 14).

15 Woman Folly presented in Proverbs is ultimately Satan himself. He seduces us with his words as in the Garden in order to get us to destroy ourselves.

16 The phrase "Israelite Dear Abby" originated with Russell Moore. His teaching on Proverbs is summarized in Appendix 1, "Walking the Line."

17 This section has been greatly aided by Longman's work on the identities of Woman Wisdom and Woman Folly. See Longman, Proverbs, 58-61.

18 I demonstrate below how Wisdom ultimately points to Jesus, but I want to also point out here that the description of Wisdom in Proverbs 9 parallels the description of the kingdom as a wedding banquet in Matthew 22 where servants are sent out to compel guests to attend the banquet.

19 I am dependent on Tremper Longman for these insights. Longman, Proverbs, 215-223.

20 This is a paraphrase of Tim Keller in his sermon "True Wisdom," http://www.gospelinlife.com/true-wisdom-5411.html. Accessed 07/09/14.

21 Goldsworthy argues that the gospel now becomes the framework through which we view the world and interpret it. Graeme Goldsworthy, The Tree of Life: Reading Proverbs Today (Sydney: aio, 1993), 22-26.

22 This may raise the question for some, "I know plenty of people who have lived wise lives and things have turned out badly for them. What should we think about that?" That concern is answered in point 10 below.

23 This is a paraphrase of Russell Moore's teaching on Proverbs. See Russ Moore, "Walking the Line," http://www.russellmoore.com/resources/proverbs/. Accessed 07/09/14.

24 See Duane Garrett, Proverbs Ecclesiastes Song of Songs, NAC (Nashville: Broadman, 1993), 57.

25 This section has been greatly helped by Waltke's argument in a section in his commentary entitled "Does Proverbs Promise Too Much." See Bruce Waltke, The Book of Proverbs Chapters 1-15, NICOT (Grand Rapids: Eerdmans, 2004), 107-109.

26 Ibid., 108.

27 See Mark Dever's discussion on Proverbs. Mark Dever, The Message of the Old Testament: Promises Made (Wheaton: Crossway, 2006), 507-526.

28 Appendix 2 maps out this approach to Proverbs.

29 The fourth example could also be considered a thematic sermon of sorts because it deals with the theme of confrontational speech in Proverbs. This sermon, however, focuses on one couplet while expanding the explanation and application with other verses on the topic from Proverbs.

30 Keller, Timothy. Counterfeit Gods: The Empty Promises of Money, Sex, and Power, and the Only Hope that Matters. New York, NY: Penguin Group, 2009, ix-x.

31 This insight comes from Bruce Waltke. The first two points of the sermon were greatly strengthened by his insights. See Waltke, Proverbs 1-15, 236-250.

32 Russell Moore, "Finding Jesus in an Anthill." http://www.russellmoore.com/2009/01/25/finding-jesus-in-an-anthill-following-christ-through-wisdom-with-money-prov-66-11/. Accessed 07/08/14. The conclusion to the sermon was also aided by Moore's insights here.

33 Roland Murphy, Proverbs, NIBC (Peabody: Hendrickson, 1999), 129.

34 You can access audio for almost all of these sermons at the Baptist21 resource page. http://www.baptisttwentyone.com/baptist21-resources/

35 There are other expository sermons that can be preached from Proverbs. You could do these in an expository series, or you could tackle these passages in a thematic series. Two such passages are: 1) Proverbs 15:30-16:15, "Your Plans and God's Plans," and 2) Proverbs 31:10-31, "The Noble Wife".

36 I did this sermon as an example of how to preach the proverbs proper in an expository and Christ-centered way. By "proverbs proper" I mean the one or two line pithy sayings. There is a way to do a sermon on seemingly random proverbs that is expository and gospel-centered. It might get monotonous if you did all of Proverbs 10-31 in this way, so I gave one sermon as an example.

19974895R00101